GONE TO LOOK FOR AMERICA

An American Wilderness Odyssey

Steve Bonham

GONE TO LOOK FOR AMERICA

An American Wilderness Odyssey

Steve Bonham

Design by Christopher Lydon.
Cover design by Alan Fernihough.

Published by Artisan Creative Ltd, Derbyshire, UK.
artisan-creative.com

Artisan Creative
Books | Recordings | Performance

ISBN (paperback) 978-1-7384035-5-4
ISBN (e-book) 978-1-7384035-6-1

Contents

Preface

I've spent most of my life on the road. Sometimes literally, guitar slung on my back and boots dusty from some trail in the Appalachians or the Sahara. And sometimes inwardly, trying to understand what makes us human and what keeps us alive inside.

I've always been curious - about people, about places, about the stories we tell ourselves and each other to make sense of it all.

I suppose I've never been much good at staying in one lane. I'm a psychologist and a musician, a writer and a wanderer. I like crossing boundaries and seeing what happens in the middle - where science meets poetry, where work meets play, where sense gives way to wonder. That's where the interesting stuff lives.

I've come to believe that life is meant to be an adventure - not necessarily a grand or glamorous one, but an honest one. I've learned more from getting lost, from the people I've met by chance, and from the moments that didn't go to plan, than from any master plan or strategy. Somewhere along the way, I've come to think of this as a kind of rewilding: finding our way back to what's alive, messy, and real in ourselves.

America has always been part of that adventure for me - a place that exists as much in the imagination as on any map. It's a land of contradictions: freedom and fear, generosity and greed, myth and truth, all tangled together.

Over the years, I've crossed it many times - by Greyhound bus, on foot through mountain trails, down dusty backroads and into small towns that never make the news. Each journey has left its mark, a thread in a larger story I've been trying to understand.

Some of those stories first appeared elsewhere - in my earlier book *A Beautiful Broken Dream*, in articles and essays written along the way, and in *American Wilderness Odyssey*, a show and album born from this same search. That show - performed with my long-time companions Christopher "The Bishop" Lydon and Kev Moore - became a kind of living version of this journey:

songs and stories woven together, part concert, part confessional, part road trip.

Those performances reminded me that storytelling, like music, only really comes alive when it's shared.

This book, *Gone to Look for America*, gathers those fragments and discoveries - old and new - into one place. It's not a travelogue, nor a history lesson, but a conversation: between past and present, between the mythic America and the one you meet in a diner at midnight.

It's about the beauty and the brokenness; the moonshine spirit that can take a few raw ingredients and conjure something fierce and luminous.

Maybe, in the end, it's about what happens when we go looking for a country - and find, somewhere along the way, a clearer sense of ourselves.

Chapter 1: Gone to Look for America

My beginning was smog. I was born in Derby, in the English Midlands. It was a black-and-white place. It didn't get colour until 1968. A place of trolleybuses, coal fires, corner stores and the Birds Bakery. And smog.

Then one day my parents bought a television and, although it was in black-and-white and small, from it, in glorious imaginary colour streamed another world. *The Dick Van Dyke Show*, *Top Cat*, *Bonanza*, *The High Chaparral*. Most of all, *Bewitched*-with a witch called Samantha who could wiggle her nose.

Samantha was the first woman, other than my mother, that I truly fell in love with. Oh, how I wished she could make my mother's dubious cabbage and mashed potatoes disappear with a twinkle of her nose.

All in all, this world, conjured from a small wooden box with a flickering screen sitting between the fireplace and the rubber plant, seemed bigger, brighter, bolder, more bountiful - and excitingly darker, more dangerous and deadly - than Derby. A world of adventure. And I was entranced by this Yankee Shangri-La.

The TV continued to be the portal to the strange other world and its darkness and its light, rich in myth, magic and malefice. I remember walking to a bus stop in town with my brother. We had been swimming at the old King Street swimming baths and were heading home. It was 1968 and in the windows of the local electrical store all the TV screens were showing the assassination of Robert Kennedy. Grey flickering figures mouthing silently the anguish of a nation.

When we got home, we found our mother in tears in the kitchen. To the then morally ambivalent mind of a 13-year-old boy this act seemed as much strange and compelling as it was sad. It was impossible to imagine anyone in a shoot-out with the pipe smoking, tedious but cuddly looking British prime minister, Harold Wilson.

And then, and by now in colour, my whole family would watch the Apollo moon flights and landings. Gathered around the television we were entranced, as for the first time, with the possible exception of the odd alien abduction, humans ventured beyond our blue skies and clouds. To circumnavigate and then land on the moon.

Guided by the neat and trim presenter James Burke, with his 'owlish' glasses and his boundless enthusiasm and curiosity we journeyed by proxy into a world almost beyond imagination whilst British newspapers fretted about the price of milk and a shortage of potatoes.

To a teenage boy it was inevitable that America with its bigness, badassness and boldness, would be more bountiful and excitingly darker, more dangerous and more deadly than Derby.

Then, at first dimly, as the obligatory guitar landed in my teenage hands, I became aware of that other American conjuration of rebellion and individuality: rock 'n' roll. I loved it from the start. It's spit-in-your-eye awkwardness, it's a willingness to bite the hand that feeds you, it's an exhilarating, unhinged sense of freedom. And the original shaman was Elvis.

Elvis? I didn't know him well. He was just there, you know, from the beginning. A citizen of another world. There from the beginning of my life, the beginning of my awareness, the beginning of my sense that there was another world.

I remember the moment he died. I was leaving my girlfriend's house, late, close to midnight. Driving home through quiet streets, I switched on Radio Luxembourg, the best rock station at the time, a lifeline of American sound in our grey English nights. A news flash broke in. Elvis Presley was dead.

Tony Prince the DJ, clearly in pieces, kept repeating: "Elvis Presley, the King of Rock 'n' Roll, has died."

By then, for me, Elvis was almost a cartoon - bloated, Vegas-suited, more myth than man. But hearing those words, something shifted. I pulled over. It was as if something foundational had gone missing, some beat behind the beat.

For those a little older than me, Elvis had been the liberator. The Beatles, the Stones, so many of that generation, spoke of the shock of first hearing him - the hips, the hair, the howl - and the sudden sense that life could be lived louder, freer, wilder. To them he was the jailbreak. By the time I came of age, he was already part of the furniture, fading into caricature. His death, though, made me look again. Beneath the rhinestones and the Vegas myth, I glimpsed the young man from Tupelo - the dirt-poor kid who carried a whole other possibility on his back.

The thing about Elvis was that he was a different kind of hero. Behind the glamour he was still an ordinary guy. Sure, he had those inciting hips and a voice that could slide from raising Cain to summoning angels, but he remained recognisably local - someone in whom an ordinary Joe or Joanne could glimpse a bit of themselves. British heroes, by contrast, always seemed to belong to another world. They were posh, rich, sophisticated, languid. They never seemed to work or worry. They could be urbane, funny, brave, even inspirational - but they could never be me.

Elvis was different. He wasn't born in silk sheets or Oxford drawing rooms. He burned his way up from nothing - raw fire, restless energy, rising from the ashes of poverty into the glare of the spotlight. He was proof that ordinary lives could flare into something extraordinary.

That, I think, lit the fuse. If he could rise from the backstreets of Tupelo, there was some weird and wonderful alchemy going on, a kind of cultural moonshining by which a few raw ingredients summon up a supernatural spirit.

And so, the search began. Not a single road trip or one-off adventure, but a lifetime of listening for that hidden rhythm. Not the America paraded on the news or hawked in glossy brochures, but an off-the-tracks, backdoor America. The one that lingers in backroads and half-forgotten songs, in the way a stranger leans across a bar to tell you their story. Not the headlines, but the silences between them. Not the big sell, but the small truths - fragile and easily missed unless you're listening hard.

It is here that the real America lies. A place born of revolution, carrying the defiance of those who resisted kings, barons and despots. A place where you are judged not by your ancestors but by the choices you make, choices that cut to the bone of who you really are. A place where, like Elvis, you might still rise to a better song.

I wrote a song later, *Midnight Radio*, to try and capture it. Not just his death, but what he had represented. How he was a totem, a vessel, for something vast and contradictory and shining: a manifestation of spirit of America.

The night the King died and the beat played on.
The world had turned; my innocence was gone.
I slipped away from the kiss of her warm bed.
I drove my car to the beat inside my head.
He hadn't meant that much to me,
But the DJ he really cried.
To a back-street boy from a Midland town
Something should have died.

Is this dream an illusion? Was it always one?

America is a shapeshifter of a place. From the outside it looks like a land of huge cities, modern highways, and corporations with the wealth of several small nations combined. The home of brands that glow in every mall in the world. A huge, interconnected superhighway of the concrete and the virtual, the standardised and the homogenous.

Its ambition - one it has just about achieved - is to plant its flag in the consciousness of every human being.

Big, brash, and crushingly dominant.

And yet, and yet… much of America is small, hometown, remote, overlooked, disconnected, and even a bit lonely. My good friend Patrick Allitt, Professor of History at Emory University, once told me the best way to think of America was as a huge wilderness with some very large conurbations dotted about. And a consequence of this, he said, was that "what we assume as a shared understanding of the world drops sharply off as you move away from these centres."

"Sure," he told me, "Atlanta is a great modern 'world' city with a very sophisticated view of how things are - but 60 miles from here you will find settlements in which people are as likely to hold to Creationism as to Darwinian evolution."

Perhaps I shouldn't, but I love this - this feeling that when you step away from the manufactured, Disney fake of a world in which the big corporations determine every sanitised, breathing moment of your lived experience, you tumble over an edge and fall headlong into another world where the thin veneer of your assumptions of how Americas is, doesn't make any sense at all. Where your map of the world is meaningless. Where people are not like you, or more pressingly, may not like you!

It's down here that for me the DNA of America emerges. From the serendipity of accidental meetings and moments. From the sons of moonshiners, in the syncopated picking of the Piedmont blues, the gas station in Nowheresville, the stamp of dancing feet in the dirt.

These small communities for me are the source of stories - the raw materials that make up the mythology of America. The settlers who founded them didn't come to America empty-handed. Alongside whatever possessions they could carry, they brought their songs, their myths, their tall tales, their scriptures - the oral luggage of their old worlds. Around campfires, in church halls, at barn dances, and later on in front porches and in pool halls, these stories were told and retold, reshaped by the new land but still carrying the rhythm and imagery of far-off places.

Some tales are long and some short. You will hear both on the road, long rambling ones in grunted sentences and others as small and shiny as a pearl.

Sometimes the stories just a line or two, redolent with implication and richness, a kind of Western Haiku.

I checked into a hotel once in Asheville. I was greeted at reception by a very grumpy owner-chef. He glared at me irritated by my arrival.

"My wife should be checking you in," he said "but she's upstairs recovering from a knee replacement. In fact, she had so much replaced over the last few years there's not much of the original left."

Tracking for a while through the Appalachian wilderness on a hot and steaming day I stopped for a while to buy a soft drink from the fishing store. I sat outside drinking it. A middle-aged man in a checked short and fishing baseball hat was sitting on the bench next to me, tapping away at a laptop. We got talking. He told me he was writing a book.

“Oh really,” I said. “Me too, what is it about?”

“I’ll tell you how it starts,” he said. “Old man Silas knew more Shakespeare than any man for over 50 miles!”

Then hitching a lift in the back of a beat-up flatbed all the way to Cherokee with two old hillbillies chatting in the front.

Charlie: “You see this corner, John? I’ve run over about twenty damn Copperheads this year, going round it.”

John: “Hell.”

Charlie: “Doesn’t do ’em much good.”

John: “Nope.”

In these pages I want to share with you my America as a weatherworn patchwork of tales, anecdotes and fables drawn from the overlooked America. I am in august company to which I cannot claim membership.

Over the years I have come to realise many of the most influential American musicians, authors, and actors of the last century came from rural or small-town backgrounds, often drawing deeply on those places for inspiration, authenticity, and a certain stubborn independence. Their roots are in a necessary cussedness and defiance and a deep sense of the community required for survival.

The soul of America doesn't just thunder from its big cities; it seeps out of small towns, porches, cotton fields, mining camps, and dusty backroads. In Tupelo, Mississippi, a poor boy in a shotgun house soaked up gospel, country, and the blues drifting north from Beale Street - and when Elvis hit the stage, all that longing and swagger erupted at once. Far to the north in Hibbing, Minnesota, a restless kid twisted the crackle of distant radio stations into songs that carried him from the frozen iron range to Greenwich Village, where Bob Dylan remade American poetry.

Down in Arkansas, Johnny Cash grew up with cotton on his hands and hymns in his ears; his voice seemed carved from the same soil he worked, carrying the weight of prisoners, farmers, and forgotten men. In the Smoky Mountains, Dolly Parton turned the hardship of a cabin without electricity into a fountain of wit, grit, and generosity, dressing her roots in rhinestones but never denying where they came from. Woody Guthrie, guitar slung across his shoulder, rode the rails out of Oklahoma, catching the voices of migrants and drifters and turning them into a manifesto: *this land is your land*. And in Oxford, Mississippi, William Faulkner proved that even the narrow gossip of a courthouse square could bloom into an entire imagined county, a mirror of America's tangled truths.

And those voices weren't only white or southern. The same story runs deep through Black America. Langston Hughes was born in Joplin, Missouri, and raised in small Midwestern towns like Lawrence, Kansas. Out of those ordinary places, he carried the hum of jazz and the ache of the blues into poems that could mourn and dream in the same breath, his words later becoming the heartbeat of Harlem. Maya Angelou, raised in the little town of Stamps, Arkansas, lifted the voices of porches and pews into a poetry of dignity and defiance, her lines carrying the weight of ordinary lives to the whole world. And in Mississippi, Robert Johnson stood at a lonely crossroads, where legend says he struck his bargain with the devil and caught the tiger of poor America by the tail.

These artists did more than make music or write novels; they remapped the country in our minds. They gave us a vision of America that wasn't all skyscrapers and neon, but homesteads and fields, dirt roads and train whistles, Sunday services and Saturday night dances.

The 'real America' they represented - or at least the one the public came to believe in - was a blend of fact and myth. It was shaped by geography and hardship, but also by the way these artists packaged their stories for a wider world. Small-town authenticity became a kind of cultural currency, especially as the country urbanised. The further America moved into suburbs and high-rises, the more it craved the voices from the edge, the ones that could claim a purer connection to the soil, to the past, to some imagined heartland.

It's a paradox, of course. The songs and novels that celebrated the unvarnished local life often reached us only after being amplified, recorded and marketed, sometimes by the very forces of mass culture they appeared to resist. But that tension between the centre and the margins, between the corporate and the homemade, is part of what makes American culture so distinctive.

So, here we go. And for sure, New Orleans, Nashville and LA loom large in my consciousness as do New York and Kansas, Atlanta and San Francisco; but it is the small places that will capture it all best. From Reliance to Lomo Parda, Troutman to the Ancient Ways cafe, from the forgotten settlement of Proctor lost in the Appalachian wilderness to the Zuni Pueblo and all the trails in between.

Welcome to the protean magic of America. It can be as vast and anonymous as a freeway at rush hour, but also as intimate and particular as a hymn sung in a church of thirty people. It's in the voices that rise from the margins, carrying with them the places that made them, and reminding us that the edges of the map are often where the heart of the country beats loudest.

Intermission: The Last Bandit

One from the bar somewhere in New Mexico. Back in the outlaw days of old Las Vegas, where Spanish-speaking bandoleros were one type of many different gangs of ne'er-do-wells getting by robbing banks, kidnapping and stealing cattle.

On one occasion, three bandits robbed a bank and made off with a bag of gold. The sheriff and a posse made off after them, killing two of them on the way. Finally, they cornered the surviving bandit in a ruined hacienda near the border. From inside the band he wouldn't back down, cursing them in Spanish and letting off a random round of ammunition if the posse got too close.

The sheriff, a careful man, got Butch, one of his followers who spoke Spanish to ask the outlaw to tell them where the money was and to surrender.

¿Dónde está el oro? shouted Butch. Where is the gold?

¡Dile que se vaya al diablo! shouted back the bandit.

"He says you can go to hell, sheriff," translated Butch.

The sheriff bridled at this. "Tell him to come out and tell me, or we'll fill him full of lead!"

Butch translated this.

¡Dile que se vaya al diablo! replied the bandit.

"He says you can still go to hell, Sheriff," said Butch.

Now the sheriff got really mad. "Tell him if he won't tell us, we'll drag him out, shoot him in both legs, then in the belly, before putting a bullet between his eyes!"

Again, the translation.

This time the bandit said: *El oro está debajo del puente que acabas de cruzar.* The gold is under the bridge you just crossed.

"He still says go to hell," said Butch.

Chapter 2: Trippin'

One of the great recurring questions of life is: when he calls do, you hear the piper on the hillside? How do you react when, unbidden, the world summons you to choose between should I stay or should I go? It is a particular moment because you realise that whichever option you take, everything has changed. Would we have heard of Columbus if he had thought: "nah, all those months bobbing around cooped up on a boat? I think I'll stay in Genoa and become a chicken farmer."

So it was, in the summer after my graduation, of having done surprisingly better than most people including me expected and as the rain poured down for days on end on a world that offered no clue onto what I might try to do next, that I suddenly remarked to my mother that if it was still raining at four o'clock this afternoon, I'm was going to go to America. I was offering my future up to the dice of fate and at four o'clock it was still raining and so I went. I sold everything I had, including my guitar, did lots of shifts as a barman, scraped together a little money and after a few weeks I was on my way.

I had a university friend in Los Angeles who had said, on the comfortable assumption that it was extremely unlikely, "If you're ever over this way, come and stay."

So, I found myself on the longest solo journey of my life. Lost and stranded in the space after education, I'd travelled to Atlanta heading for California - landing there not because of planning, but because I couldn't afford a ticket all the way to Los Angeles. All I had was a one-way Greyhound ticket and fifty dollars in my pocket.

From the airport, I went straight to the Greyhound station. My memory paints it in an Art Deco style, humid as hell, well past midnight. Crude metal benches bolted to the floor. On one, a black woman sat, head tilted, gently stroking the hair of a young girl asleep across her lap. Two suspicious-looking young men leaned on a Coca-Cola vending machine. An old man sat on the floor nearby, crying quietly, plastic carrier bags at his feet. That was the scene I stepped into.

Boarding that Greyhound and setting off across America - through Georgia, Tennessee, Arkansas, Texas, Arizona - was one of the great trips of my life. For 60 hours, America passed by in a dusty, dreamlike sequence. I stood on the corner in Winslow, Arizona, right there on Route 66, feeling like I had fallen into a Chuck Berry song. The names of towns came and went like verses, places both lyrically familiar and utterly strange. The memory fades but Montgomery, Jackson, Dallas, El Paso, Phoenix and Tucson linger on.

Somewhere around Little Rock, a girl with long dark hair got on the bus and asked if she could sit next to me. We didn't talk much - it was late, and we were both drifting - but just before we nodded off to sleep, she offered me a stick of Wrigley's gum. As the lights of oncoming trucks flickered across the bus's interior, we both fell into a rhythm of movement and rest. When I awoke in the dim grey dawn over the tobacco fields, her head was resting gently on my shoulder. Sometime later, I came to again, groggy and uncertain, and she was gone. All that remained was the memory of her cool hair against my cheek and a fresh piece of gum she'd left for me wrapped in its paper and foil.

The bus hardly stopped except to clean or change vehicles. We travelled through fields of soybeans, corn, cotton, wheat. Miles followed trance-like miles. It was hypnotic. Round and round in my head, on an endless loop, ran Jim Morrison's louche, enigmatic voice:

"Oh, moon of Alabama / We now must say goodbye / We've lost our good old mama / And must have whiskey, oh, you know why."

Eventually getting to Los Angeles I was rescued by my old friend Peter Schwarz and driven to stay in his father's house in the Hollywood Hills - I felt like a cheapskate version of the legendary Oisín arriving into Tír na nÓg ('the Land of Eternal Youth').

Like millions before I had headed west and arrived.

Long before Kerouac's scrolls or Fonda's chopper, the road west was already myth. The wagon trains creaked across the Santa Fe Trail, whole families staking their lives on the promise that the horizon held salvation. Later Guthrie sang through dustbowl towns, Steinbeck's Joads rattled toward California in jalopies heavy with hope. The road was never just asphalt - it was redemption, renewal, the belief that movement itself could remake a life. Even the cars became symbols: Bel Airs, Mustangs, Eldorados - freedom forged in chrome and steel. Always, though, the shadow travelled with them: Depression families, their beds and guitars lashed to battered Hudsons, chasing survival more than romance. Yet whether out of necessity or desire, every journey carried the same possibility - that on the road, you might be transformed.

I wasn't fleeing famine or chasing fortune, but somewhere in that Greyhound rumble was a whisper of the same truth: that movement changes us. That Greyhound from Atlanta to Los Angeles wasn't just a ride west; it was a kind of initiation. I didn't know it then, but something in me was waking up. Maybe it was the endless miles of cotton fields and desert, maybe it was the strange fellowship of strangers squeezed together for days on end. But I began to realise I wasn't just travelling - I was witnessing. Taking it in. Filing away scraps of story. I was absorbing and being absorbed. I was discovering *withinness*.

Withinness is the moment the world stops being scenery and starts becoming part of your own undertow, pulling you inward, moving from outside to inside, soaking into your bones with its smells, its noise, even its grit.

Many travellers never reach that state. They skate across the surface of places that have been carefully tidied for their arrival - the cultural cushions plumped up on the sofa, the bric-a-brac locked away, the unsavoury swept out of sight. And so, instead of the undertow, they settle for the shallows: the sanitised hotels, the air-conditioned coaches, the cruise ships - a tour of bright shadows, while the real life of the place runs unseen beneath their feet...

On that bus you didn't get the America of brochures or news bulletins. You got the raw stuff: the soldier on leave, the runaway with a bag of nothing much, the grandmother with her paper sack of sandwiches. Ordinary folk, each carrying a hidden world. I started to see that this was the real map of America - not the road atlas, but the people themselves.

I remember one stop at three in the morning in Alabama. The bus pulled up at a town that seemed half-asleep, just a scattering of neon buzzing against the dark. We shuffled out into the hot, wet air, blinking, stiff-legged. The place smelled of fried grease and diesel. Inside the station café, a few of us ordered coffee so thin you could almost see through it.

I sat across from a guy in an army jacket; his name stitched in fading thread. He was on leave, heading home, though he didn't sound too sure he wanted to get there. He spoke in half-sentences, the way people do when they're carrying something heavy in their chest. Next to us, a woman with a shopping bag of sandwiches quietly slid one to a young lad who looked like he hadn't eaten for a while. No one said much about it. Then the driver barked "ten minutes," and just like that we all shuffled back into the dark belly of the Greyhound.

It was nothing, really. Just a brief stop in a nowhere town. But I carried it with me - the sense that every seat on that bus held a story you'd never fully know; that America wasn't in the headlines but in these fleeting, human exchanges at three in the morning.

Looking back, I think that Greyhound was where the outline of me first appeared: wanderer, musician, storyteller. And quietly, an observer of the human theatre passing by.

That's the thing about American roads. They're not just strips of tarmac. They're highways of dreams. A line on a map is never just a border - it's the point where you decide who you are. No wonder American movies keep returning to the road trip: rite of passage, desperate escape, comic disaster, spiritual pilgrimage. The road trip *is* the American dream in motion - the hope that somewhere down the line, you can begin again.

It's not about A to B. It's about what happens in between. What shakes loose. What gets left behind. Who you become along the way.

And sometimes the road just makes you laugh at the sheer madness of it all. Years later, I was driving through Tennessee when the road gave me one of its stranger gifts: I started to notice the billboards. Not the national brands for tyres, sodas, or burgers - though there were plenty of those - but the local ones. The grinning real estate agents. The shiny lawyers promising justice. The preachers offering salvation. They all looked the same. Perhaps they were.

Maybe it was the film *Three Billboards Outside Ebbing, Missouri* that set me looking at them in sets of three. Because one day, somewhere down the road, this sequence appeared:

"Automatic and semiautomatic rifles - weekly and weekend rates." A second's reflection on the madness of gun control.

Followed by: "Cremations with confidence!" leading to a bit self-inquiry on exactly what you might want to feel confident about.

And finally: "Catholic sex shop ... take early exit!" That good old Catholic birth control salsa. 1 - 2 - 3 - STOP!

Three lines, a whole moral universe...

On another trip, from Las Vegas to New Mexico I drove, according to the song Route 66 backwards - Kingman, Flagstaff, Gallup - with a little *Take It Easy* thrown in, stopping in Winslow, Arizona. The Mother Road, America's main street, stretched out ahead of us: long ribbons of asphalt stitched across flat plains, the horizon marked by rust-red cliffs and sage-covered mesas, as though an ancient basilica had been carved into the bones of the desert.

I stopped for a rest in Seligman, a place surviving on memory rather than momentum. Wooden-veranda stores peddled Route 66 T-shirts, copper jewellery, gun-shop kitsch, faded portraits of John Wayne and James Dean. Inside the Road Runner Café we met Paula - weather-worn, tall hat, a laugh like dry wind. She made copper jewellery and was terrified of rattlesnakes. Her husband was a gold prospector. She told us she once painted a piece of wood gold and planted it in his pan.

"He thought he'd struck it rich," she grinned.

"Still married?" I asked.

"Thirty years. He stays for the cooking."

And then there were the motels... the bastions and sanctuaries of the great American highway.

Forget the Empire State Building, the Golden Gate Bridge, the French Market in New Orleans, the Statue of Liberty, Disney World or even the Grand Canyon. Nothing is more exotic to this Englishman, pulling in off the highway, than a homemade, all-American motel. Take the trail across the USA and you may see many things, but one is certain: sooner or later, caught in the glare of a Ford pickup's headlights, under flickering neon in the shimmering heat, you will find a motel.

Beware imitations. Foreign knockoffs don't count. The genuine article is distinctly American. It's a refuge for the fugitive, the loner, the midnight assignation, the restless salesman, the runaway housewife. You sleep behind quadruple-locked doors, pointlessly beside big easy-push-in windows, lulled by a clanking aircon unit that rattles like a train and competes with a TV screen the size of a football pitch. Two beds, both vast enough to host a five-a-side match, dominate a room so long that daylight never reaches the mirrored far wall. In the gloom is always a celebration of the art of packaging, everything comes in little packets: coffee, creamer, sugar, soap. But this collection of consumables is but the *amuse bouche* to the main event, the motel breakfast where your post prandial conscience is pricked by looking at the mountain on the table in front of you of empty packets, wrappers and cartons of jam, butter, waffle batter, cream cheese, paper cups, paper plates, and plastic knives, forks and spoons.

More than a few of the motels I have stayed in have come with that frisson of threat around who exactly your fellow guests might be, Amongst those arriving in beat up old trucks, old Dodgers and the inevitable Ford, more than a few look like they are part of a Witness Protection Programme and the rest might have stashed a body in the trunk.

And then there are owners. You half-expect Anthony Perkins to come round with a towel.

The Bates Motel in *Psycho* has become the cultural shorthand for all that is dodgy about roadside lodging. The 'vacancy' sign flickers just a shade too ominously, the manager greets you with a smile that is 70% friendly, 30% serial killer, and the shower comes with a complimentary existential crisis. Thanks to Norman Bates, we've all absorbed the rule: if a motel looks too cheap, too remote, or too quiet, it's probably not your imagination. It's your cue to run. His legacy? A whole genre of horror movies, a whole etiquette of road travel - and the habit of checking behind the shower curtain before you dare brush your teeth.

And reality is closer to this than you think. Kev, an old friend and bass player in my band, was touring in the southern states and he returned to his motel one evening to find flashing blue lights and a cordoned-off room. His room, as it happened, was right next door. With some trepidation, he approached, only to be stopped by an officer, while colleagues quietly carried out a body bag. The questions came sharp and official: his name, his whereabouts between eight and ten. There had, indeed, been a murder in the room beside his. Kev, mercifully, had a watertight alibi. He hunkered down for the night - though 'sleep' might not be quite the right word.

That's the thing about America. Out on the road, reality and the movies aren't distant cousins. They're travelling companions. And the motel, for all its neon promises, is a reminder of the double-edged spirit of the road: part freedom, part danger, part comedy, part fear. Like the country itself, it never lets you settle.

The myth - of departure, transformation, reinvention - has powered America's imagination for centuries. You hear it in the music too. I once wrote a song myself, *Riding on the Road That Never Ends.* It came from a moment, but it touched something timeless:

In a Studebaker '61 that smells of oil and dust,
A beat-up old convertible,
whose soul is made of rust.
Ride Jenny and her lover,
laughing as they're chasing trains,
He's got his foot down hard, going like a hurricane.

The song winds through the same landscapes I'd travelled: railways, prairies, lost highways, dusty borders. It spoke to the bittersweet blur of motion, where love and longing ride in the same seat, and freedom is always one stop, one kiss, one story away.

Because the road isn't just a place. It's a spell. A road that never really ends. Whether behind the wheel of a Buick or slouched in a bus seat watching the blue-stemmed grass, you couldn't help but feel you were part of something larger. That maybe, just maybe, redemption was only a few hundred miles away.

And that, I suppose, is the heart of it. Call it searching, call it running, call it dreaming. For me it was simply trippin' - and I've never stopped.

Intermission: This Strange Motel

Jim watches some old show, drinks his coffee on repeat.
Whichever way he goes along a losing street.
Someone's shouting out aloud, the police out here are
  trying to frame me.
Just a face in an angry crowd, someone come and save me.

  Out on the highway, this heart-worn carousel.
  We're all seeking refuge, in this strange motel.

In the room across the hall, sleeps the lonely Madeleine.
All her hopes are in a hold all, life like a weather vane.
Joe and Sue are making love, he's never seen a girl so naked.
Gives his thanks to the Lord above, he found this room vacated.

Jean folds up her party dress, placed it slowly in a suitcase.
Starts to think it's for the best, she quits this hiding place.
As the card school starts to go, getting ice from on the landing.
Ace or deuce it's hard to know, it takes some understanding.

Listen online: arcr.uk/gtlfamusic

Chapter 3: Trekkin'

What is the speed of discovery? This is a question. How slow do you have to go to be truly in a place, rather than just marching through it? Of course, one answer might be: don't move at all. Just stand still and let the world come to you - something I too often forget. But then again, not moving rather limits the range of possibilities.

On the other extreme, maximum speed - like flying - is a concertina of distance and time in which richness and diversity simply evaporate. So, slow walking pace is the speed of deep discovery. Sauntering, if you will. The average speed of an ox-drawn wagon train heading out west along the Oregon or Santa Fe trails was two to three miles an hour. A team of horses might manage three or four, maybe six on a perfect day.

But a team of horses ain't so strong, and you might have to leave the sideboard or the grandfather's clock back in Independence or Kansas City.

Ten miles in a day is respectable. Fifteen is killing it. On a forced march, Roman legionnaires might hit thirty. But at that pace all you really notice is the state of your feet. So, there you have it: the natural and historically correct way to discover America is at walking pace. At this pace, the country unfolds. And more than just the landscape emerges. You meet people. You stop and talk for a while. A vignette, a rendezvous. And you begin to sense the ghosts of those who walked before you, and the elemental connection to your ancestors.

Walking into the Appalachians, I thought often about those who had come before. Long before Greyhounds, railways, or even wagons, America was entered step by step. The ancestors of the Pueblo peoples, and of so many others, crossed the land bridge from Asia at the end of the Ice Age on foot, carrying their lives on their backs, following the herds into a continent they had never seen. The footpath, not the wheel, was the beginning of American history.

Those trails deepened into a web across the continent. Some became sacred routes, carved into sandstone mesas by the Pueblo peoples, still visible today. Others carried trade: turquoise mined in New Mexico turned up in the Great Plains; shells from the Gulf Coast appeared in Ohio Valley villages. All of it, every mile, moved on foot. To walk was to survive, to carry stories, to keep families fed and connected.

When the Spanish reintroduced horses in the sixteenth century, everything changed, but only partly. Some tribes, like the Lakota or the Comanche, transformed themselves into horse nations. They became riders without equal. But even then, most of the world still moved at the pace of legs. Horses were precious, to be saved for hunting or fighting. Camps and possessions moved as they always had: one step at a time.

And when the Europeans pushed west with their wagons, they too mostly walked. The Hollywood version shows families riding proudly on the buckboard, but the reality was dust and blisters. Wagons crawled at two miles an hour, the speed of a tired walker. Oxen strained, wheels groaned, and inside was no place to ride - the jolting was brutal. So, men, women, and children trudged beside the wheels. Diaries from the Oregon Trail are full of complaints about raw feet, broken shoes, and exhaustion. America was settled as much by calluses as by courage.

The traces are still there. On the Santa Fe Trail, you can see the wagon ruts carved into the prairie, etched not only by wheels but by the millions of footsteps alongside them. On mesas in the Southwest, you can find sandstone worn smooth by centuries of bare feet. Even here in Appalachia, I stumbled across old chimneys or gravestones, the last signs of people who had walked their way into these woods with all they owned.

Walking is slow, but it is also intimate. It presses you into the land in a way nothing else can. Settlers may have cursed every mile, but they came to know the feel of clay after rain, the smell of crushed pine needles, the sound of streams that had to be crossed again and again. On foot you don't pass through a place; you are claimed by it.

And so, it seems only right that if you want to look for America you do at least part of it on foot. Not the whole country - I'm not that mad - but a good, solid stretch of it. Springer Mountain in Georgia is where the mighty Appalachian Trail begins, two thousand miles of footsore determination all the way to Maine. But I set my boots instead on the Benton MacKaye Trail, named after the man who first dreamed up the idea of the Appalachian Trail. His version was less travelled, less tamed, a wilder parallel through the forests of Georgia, Tennessee, and North Carolina. And to be fair a whole lot shorter - about 300 or so miles. That sounded about right for me.

I wanted to know what it felt like to walk into the unknown, into the wilderness, as millions had before me. To carry my world on my back, to measure time not by the clock but by the rise and fall of the trail. To let the land dictate the rhythm. That's the idea of through-hiking: you don't dip in and out; you surrender to the trail until it becomes your whole world.

It was a strange time to begin. I had set out with my companion sandwiched between two hurricanes sweeping up from the Gulf of Mexico, clawing talons of rain and wind reaching deep inland. The ground was slick, the air heavy, and the woods themselves seemed restless.

The Benton MacKaye does not make things easy. Blowdowns - huge trees brought down by past storms - forced me to scramble, to climb, to crawl under. Humidity clung to me like a wet shirt that never dried. Spiders spun webs across the trail, invisible until they wrapped themselves across my face, their angry architects dangling from the brim of my hat. Then came the caterpillars: one stretch where hundreds of the green things rained down from the branches like a biblical plague.

There were bears, too - mostly unseen, but always present in the imagination.

And yet, there was something mesmerising about it. The trail twisted like a roller coaster, throwing me up and down ridges, in and out of shadow. I carried my world on my back, filtering water from muddy pools, eating where I could, sleeping where I dropped. Slowly the noise of the outside world fell away. The trail began to set the rhythm of my days. And you start to notice things. The bear scratches on the tree, an amiable turtle walking through the damp undergrowth, the funnel-shaped webs being woven above your head. The smaller things. I came to a small clearing. I lit a little fire and sat down to write my diary by headtorch. It was then I noticed, carved into the trunk of a fallen white oak tree, the letters:

D♡BM

"Duane loves Billy Marie," perhaps.

A small declaration, scrawled into the wilderness. The ghosts of other wanderers, lovers, fellow travellers, leaving their own mark as if to say: *we were here, too*.

Lying by the fire that night, I invented them as young lovers guarded by an old black bear under a creaking pine, serenaded by coyotes singing in the dark. This turned into our song, *The Ballad of Duane and Billy Marie.*

Another storm swept inland, and my companion and I were forced off the trail toward a roadhead. With the trees groaning in the wind and the rain closing in, I managed to find a signal, call a hotel in Blue Ridge, and arrange for a ride. That's how I met Everett.

Now, most taxi drivers I've met - and this is a global observation - operate somewhere between apoplexy and despair. In New York they are gloriously rude, in Hong Kong frosty as ice, and in Bucharest possessed of a death wish that involves overtaking mules and Russian trucks at the same time. Everett? Everett laughed the whole time.

He wasn't really a taxi driver at all, but a nature photographer living alone in a log cabin with a cat that had been bitten twice by rattlesnakes and survived. After that, the cat preferred the roof, which was understandable, since a mountain lion had once tried to come in through the back door.

As he drove us into Blue Ridge ahead of the storm, and back out again when it had passed, Everett pointed out rare plants and birds from the driver's seat, encyclopaedic in his knowledge of the backwoods. The common stuff and the rare stuff.

"You never what you're gonna meet out here next," he said.

Strange people too, I replied. Like Teepee Walter, who we had bumped into a few days earlier, hanging around outside his large orange tent in the middle of nowhere. I wasn't sure why Walter was 'TeePee'. Perhaps it was a reference to his fluorescent tent. He obviously wasn't through-hiking with it – it was far too big. Instead, he was using it as base camp from which he could do a series of day hikes. He'd been there since the snows, gradually ticking off various routes and paths. I got the feeling he was getting weary of the work but felt compelled to do them all in that way that a slight and transient goal can morph into an existential crisis.

I also told Everett that I had been somewhat knocked off balance by the need to always wear something bright and fluorescent in case an over-enthusiastic hunter mistakes you for a deer.

"They scare me, man," Everett said of the hunters. "They get themselves some cases of beer and boxes of ammo, take the kids out and just go shooting at everything - even the trees."

"Hunters ain't the only problem though. People use the depths of the woods for all kinds of stuff they shouldn't."

"You always know when you've stumbled over the bad'uns, they don't use their names so you can't identify them."

"You've got to be real careful with those guys," he told me. "If I come across them, I just say I'm taking nature photographs - and act like I think they're doing the same, whatever the evidence to the contrary."

Once, he said, he stumbled into a clearing full of them, his camera in hand.

"What ya doin' here?" asked one of the men, swaying with a rifle in one hand and a beer in the other. The others behind him were digging a large hole. Next to it a suspicious looking black bag lay on the ground.

"Taking photographs of flowers," said Everett, truthfully but disingenuously. "Don't suppose you've seen a pink Moccasin

Flower have you - pink thing, shaped like a Moccasin of course, very rare, grows hereabouts in the leaf litter?"

The man rocked back and forth, chewing this over, then called out: "Hey Wayne, have you seen any stuff round here that looks like a pink moccasin? Wayne, looking mighty pissed at being identified, said he had not."

When the storm had blown itself out, Everett dropped us back on the trail. The Benton MacKaye still had no mercy. A tremendous amount of water had fallen over the previous few days and the recovering heat made the mist rise from the ground and the undergrowth as if the land had been holding its breath. It was as muggy as an old Chinatown steamy and the branches of bushes and smaller trees, heavy with moisture, hung like great, green pantaloons. Woodpeckers, disgruntled and damp, would hammer out sudden angry loud double paradiddles into the cosmos.

The going was so remorseless even I couldn't help wondering what it would have been like to arrive here from rural England, a few hundred years ago and stand with your family and think: this is my world, and I had better start making it. What character and culture would be hammered out here in a place that was so remote and support far away?

And yet, long before those settlers came with their axes and their prayers, others had already called this land home - the Cherokee and their ancestors, who had walked these same ridges and valleys for centuries, naming the rivers, mapping the seasons, reading the forest as a living text. To them, this wasn't wilderness to be conquered but a vast, breathing companion - a world to be lived *with*, not *against*. It's hard to imagine what they thought, watching strangers stumble in, mistaking survival for ownership.

Now and then in a clearing of by the trail I would find a little gravestone or marker of those who had arrived and failed. Most poignant of all after days without seeing a sign of anyone, we found a clearing, with a small chapel open to the wind and a handful of graves looking out across the endless forest. Most belonged to three families: the Pattersons, the Milsops, and the Dyers. Some stones simply read *infant*. Somehow the graves were still tended, plastic flowers scattered by storms.

After ten days in the forests, having run out of water and being seriously dehydrated, I was deeply trail sick. We made our way off a long ridge and found our way to one of those wonderful unsupervised campsites that the state provides for the more adventurous camper.

The campsite was just about empty but near the entrance sat by a fire beside a Toyota Land Cruiser sat a round-faced, curly-haired guy in his mid-twenties. I dropped onto the concrete picnic bench beside him, trying to remember how to speak.

He passed me a tin mug of iced water.

“Best thing for dehydration,” he said. Then handed me an ice-cold Dr Peppers.

Till the day I die, that will be the finest drink I’ve ever tasted.

His name was Pat - a barman between jobs, out here on his own with a barbecue, cooler, and a cigar-box guitar. “If you tune that for me,” he grinned, “I’ll cook you supper.”

And he did. Gnocchi, salad, burgers, orange juice. I hadn’t eaten properly in a week. We sat by the fire swapping stories - travels, jobs, songs - and later I played a few chords while he smoked pot through an apple.

He came from a place in Florida once called Boggy Bayou, renamed - by the postmaster’s daughter, no less - *Niceville*. Somehow that seemed to fit him: kind, open, hopeful.

Next day we got to a little place called Reliance on the Hiwassee River. Emerging from the dappling darkness of the trees I was confronted by a site of breathtaking loveliness. The sparkling river ran through a narrow green plain from which wooded hills rose steeply on either side. There was a road, the first I had seen for days, winding its way along one side.

Reliance is not really a place. It’s more random spread of settlements, the principal one of which is the Webb Brother store and gas station.

If you distilled every image of rural 1950s America you would get the Webb Brothers Store on the Hiwassee river. Two incredibly old Texaco pumps stand wearily in the heat. A bruised metal sign saying 'US mail' is nailed over the door, and an old neon Coca-Cola sign flickers half-heartedly. The shop sells grits, bullets, fishing tackle, milk and lonely souvenirs.

I knew I had to come off the trail and rest up for a few days. I found somewhere to stay, thanks to the help of Eve who worked in the store. My companion pressed on without me and I hung out mostly around the store for a couple of days dozing in an old leather chair by the front door, drinking Dr Pepper and checking in with the locals.

Deciding I should move on. I decided to take a time out and head to Cherokee, a few hundred miles away, before coming back to rejoin the trail a little further on. Looking for help I went to the store.

It was there I was confronted by the remoteness of America.

I asked Eve about the possibility of catching a bus to somewhere. To anywhere!

"We've not had a bus for 20 years," she told me.

"Is there a train?" I asked. I had noticed there was a train line running along the valley.

"Not since the 1950s," she said.

By now one or two other locals had gathered out of mild interest and willingness to help.

“What about a taxi?”

“That would cost you over $200!”

Perhaps I could hitchhike, I wondered.

There was a collective intake of breath and headshaking.

“I certainly wouldn’t be doing that!” someone said.

“Why not?” I asked.

“You never know who might pick you up, there’s some mighty strange folk round here. People who might not like you!”

I had the sudden uncomfortable thought that the last person who attempted to hitch was found hanging upside down from a tree with a bullet in his head.

Yes, Reliance had shadows. Feral gangs in the back hills were cooking up crystal meth, fuelled by painkillers and despair. People worked three jobs just to survive. No trust in government, no safety net.

According to Harold Webb, the gentle owner of the store and the accommodation I was staying in, these days roaming among the bears and rattlesnakes, there were now monstrous hybrids of Russian and American boar - eight hundred pounds of tusked bad temper tearing through the underbrush.

I did get out thanks to local kindness and after a few days rejoined the trail where it swept toward the Smokies, at Fontana Dam, that vast concrete wall holding back the Little Tennessee River, and gateway to one of the Smokey Mountains National Park through which ran to its conclusion the Benton Mackay Trail.

The weather was cooler and we made good progress. Fall was just appearing at the margins of the day. Along the trail were the signs of those who went before: more gravestones, the sentinel-like chimney stacks of old cabins, an old car with a tree growing though it. The path led us toward Proctor, once a logging town, now an abandoned shell. A ghost town reclaimed by vines and silence.

And then came the bears.

The signs were everywhere - clawed trunks, berry-rich scat, a musky tang that said unseen eyes were watching. Then, rounding a slope, my companion froze. Not far off stood a black bear, broad and dark against the green. He paused, looked straight at us - not afraid, not threatening, just curious.

For a moment it felt like an exchange, a quiet recognition. Not hunter and hunted, not intruder and owner, just two creatures sharing the same ground. Then he turned and vanished into the trees.

I whooped, punched the air, and the forest seemed to smile back: a little further on, a great elk stepped across the path, antlers flashing in the light. The wilderness had spoken. I wasn't travelling any more. I was in.

I never did make the whole of the Benton Mackay. In the end, it wasn't a bear or a storm that stopped me. It was time, and my own choices. My pack had been far too heavy from the start. I had carried too much, ignored the wisdom of the light-footed. Every unnecessary pound had bitten deeper with each mile. The weather, the exhaustion, the poor kit decisions - together they wore me down until finishing became impossible.

I had to admit defeat. I had simply run out of time.

But it wasn't a bitter defeat. It was the kind that leaves a scar and knowing. Walking the Benton MacKaye Trail had taught me something I should have known all along: carry less. Not just in rucksacks, but in life. Every unnecessary weight slows you down. Strip it back, and you'll find the essentials - water, food, fire, shelter, companionship, and, if you're lucky, the glance of a bear in the Smokies.

I found the ghosts of that long journey into America still there. Chimneys where cabins once stood, wagon ruts etched into the earth, a gravestone for a lost child, a heart carved into the trunk of a fallen oak. Each mark said the same thing: *we were here, we endured.*

I found the wild itself still whispering. The webs that draped across my face at dawn, the rain steaming from the ground, the sudden hush that meant a bear was nearby. And when one finally appeared, solid and black and utterly unbothered by my small existence.

I found, too, the overlooked America - in the small kindness of a stranger with cold water and Dr Pepper; in Everett the laughing photographer with his snake-bitten cat; in Teepee Walter chasing his own strange pilgrimage. Ordinary people, improvising, surviving, making it up as they go.

And I learned some things along the way.

That discovery only happens at the pace of your own footsteps. That out here, self-reliance isn't a motto but a necessity - sometimes noble, sometimes brutal. That the weight you carry, in your pack or in your heart, will defeat you if you don't learn to put some of it down.

So yes, I found a few answers.

This America, it turns out, isn't a polished dream or a slogan on a bumper sticker. It's raw, restless, hand-built - still under construction. It's the calloused hands and the stubborn hearts of people who keep walking, even when the path disappears.

And maybe that's the lesson.

If you really want to know a place, or yourself, you have to walk until the noise falls away and the ghosts catch up. Then, when the trail runs out, you shoulder what matters, leave the rest behind, and keep on going.

Intermission: The Problem with Bears

Before I had left on my trek, everyone – well, many people - when I had told them that my intentions were to walk through the forests of Tennessee and North Carolina along the rarely visited Benton Mackay Trail, didn't ask about my goals: to explore the land of the Cherokee nation; to experience what it means to truly carry your means of survival through the wilderness; to search out, in my own little way, the soul of America.

No, virtually the only conversation was to give me their thoughts on "the Bear Problem".

About Black bears: how dangerous they were, how unpredictable, how very unafraid of humans they have become.

How very lucky I was they were only *black* bears. They might have been *grizzlies*, which, people earnestly told me, were much, much worse. (People who had never strayed beyond seeing a glass-eyed bear on the edge of their pillow, however…)

And then came the stream of advice.

Stand your ground and look big. Shout. Speak quietly but firmly. Make sure you're not between a mother bear and her cubs. Shoot them. Hang your food bag high up in the trees so they can't climb up and get it. Wear different clothes to sleep in than you've cooked in. Leave the latter at least 100 m away from wherever you're sleeping. Bears have a surprising interest in personal hygiene and your toothbrush and toothpaste, plus any soaps and wet wipes, should be hung in the tree with the food as well.

The best and most cynical advice was to not mess around… and run like hell!

And then with the theatrical pause…

"Bears can run at 30 miles an hour, so you won't escape, but at least you'll feel you are doing something useful before it grabs you and tears you to pieces."

Towards my departure date, the advice by text, email and Facebook messages steadily mounted, along with more suggestions, well-wishes and prayers etc.

“Surely,” I thought, “I can’t have that many friends that have come across bears or researched their behaviour and psychology?”

Two nights before I left, I was playing a gig. When introducing a new song I had written about America, I good naturedly grumbled about this stream of expertise and joked: “Please! No more advice about bears!”

Blow me, at the interval, someone came up to me and said, “I know you said you’d quite a lot of advice about bears...”

“No,” I said, “I said I had had *too much* advice about bears and couldn’t take any more.”

“Well, anyway,” he went on, “a good idea I heard was to...”

Chapter 4: Moonshining

In my more rambling moments, I think I might suggest in a kind of philosophical, leaning on the bar kind of way, that if the spirit of America can be represented by anything, it might be by the notion of moonshine. It's the DIY spit-in-your-eye essence of the frontier character. You take a few raw ingredients, barley, rye, water, yeast, and conjure up some raw magic. And this is a recipe for so much else. Building a cabin, singing your own song, delivering dangerous justice to a new nation.

It starts in the dark. The moon is high but the trees are higher, casting long shadows over the twisting backroads of Wickes County. Somewhere deep in those woods, a souped-up '40 Ford Coupe roars into life. Its mufflers have been doctored to keep the noise down, but the sound still rattles through the still night like a dare. Inside: one driver, hands tight on the wheel, eyes wide. The boot is full: two hundred gallons of white lightning, each jug carefully stowed and padded against the curves. Behind him, headlights flash in the distance. The revenuers. He's got ten miles of dirt and danger before the state line. And he's not slowing down for anyone.

That's moonshine.

You can't understand America without understanding moonshine. And I don't just mean the drink, though that's a hell of a place to start. I mean the spirit behind it: liberty, rebellion and the pursuit of cussedness. The stubborn determination to thrive on your own terms. It's a jar of firewater passed around under the stars, a bootleg run through mountain backroads, a raised finger to the powers that be. It says, push off, leave us alone. You really don't want us, and we really don't need you. All your ledgers, your regulations, and your permissions - moonshine is mischief in liquid form. Improvisation over regulation, craft over compliance, self-reliance over submission.

Every hidden still was proof that something potent could be conjured from the overlooked and the ignored. And here is the paradox: the very roots of this country were born of rebellion. The very institutions which sought to suppress moonshine were themselves the former agents of rebellion, and you might argue they were initially fuelled by it.

Moonshine is more than corn liquor. It's a metaphor with a kick.

It's a rough and rustic brew, brought from farmsteads and cabins and wild places by settlers from Europe. It's a people's choice. A history of the battle of ordinary folk against their self-appointed betters. It was *Poitín* in Ireland, *Slivovitz* in the dark forests of Central Europe, hedge-whisky in England, made from leftover barley. Sacks of rye past their best, potatoes or even sugar beet.

The first time I ever encountered it was being given a bottle of poteen by the son of a policeman in the Dublin Constabulary. That was in the days when the boys used to round up the known poteen stills around Dublin just before Christmas, when poteen was still illegal. They would destroy all the bad stuff, some of the good, but kept quite a lot of the best, in case the cold winter nights, cold nights, overtook them.

Opening it at home on a December evening in front of the fire, we passed the bottle around as we played old songs and tunes until the night melted into the dawn. As I staggered about the next morning assessing the damage and making a half-hearted attempt to clear up, I found the fiddle player passed out on the sitting room floor. He opened one eye, looked at me balefully and enquired:

"Why does my mouth taste of potatoes?"

Down the years, it's been the drink of choice for the independent, the isolated, and the irrepressible. Homemade, argumentative stuff you shared with your neighbour.

And, of course, that meant the government hated it.

Governments have always had it in for moonshine. Not because of the dangers (though there were a few), but because it was the three Us the authorities fear most: Unregulated. Uncontrolled and Untaxed. They wanted their cut. They employed 'Revenuers', Excise Men and the delightfully names 'Gougers' to make sure homemade fun stayed strictly off limits.

Moonshiners, meanwhile, wanted to be left alone. What followed, inevitably, was conflict. This wasn't a hobby like knitting or reading Charles Dickens - it was a two-fingered salute to authority. It said, push off, leave us alone. You really don't want us, and we really don't need you, nor your ledgers, your regulations, and your permissions. Moonshine is mischief in liquid form. Improvisation over regulation, craft over compliance, self-reliance over submission.

Every hidden still was proof that something potent could be conjured from the overlooked and the ignored. And here is the paradox: America is a place born of rebellion, so the institutions which sought to suppress moonshine were themselves the former agents of rebellion, and you might argue they were initially fuelled by it.

The irony is glorious. Moonshine was the drink of choice for the American rebels during the War of Independence-something to steel the nerve before facing the Redcoats. But once the war was won, and the British kicked out, the brand-new American government decided it needed revenue. So what did they tax? Moonshine.

The result was the Whiskey Rebellion of 1791-1794. Farmers in western Pennsylvania - many of them war veterans - rebelled violently against the federal government's new excise tax on distilled spirits.

The very government they had fought to establish was now squeezing them for survival. The tax, introduced under Alexander Hamilton's financial plan, disproportionately affected small producers in the frontier states who often used whiskey as barter currency. To them, it wasn't just taxation; it was betrayal. The King had been about taxing tea - now it was much more serious!

The resistance was fierce. Tax collectors were tarred and feathered. Federal agents were attacked. It came to a head in 1794 when several thousand insurgents gathered in rebellion. President George Washington responded with surprising severity. He personally led 13,000 militia into Pennsylvania to put down the uprising - the first and only time a sitting US president has led troops in the field. The rebels scattered, the rebellion fizzled, but the message was clear: the state would claim its share, even from its own.

Moonshine didn't die with the Whiskey Rebellion. If anything, it became more embedded in American life - particularly in the backwoods, where defiance had deep roots. It also became even more essential during another great American psychodrama: Prohibition.

From 1920 to 1933, the United States attempted to outlaw the manufacture, sale, and transportation of alcohol entirely. The 18th Amendment, enforced by the Volstead Act, turned tens of thousands of ordinary people into criminals overnight. And once again, moonshine flourished.

If the Whiskey Rebellion was about independence, Prohibition was about resistance. Speakeasies, bootleggers, and backwoods stills exploded across the country. Appalachian distillers who had long practised the craft illegally became cultural icons - men and women who kept the spirit (and spirits) alive in the face of the dry crusade. The moonshiners adapted, innovated, and expanded. And once again, the government struggled to catch up.

The 18th amendment was eventually repealed in 1933 with the 21st Amendment. Prohibition ended, but moonshining didn't die. Back in those days, making moonshine was as much a necessity as it was an act of defiance. In places like Wilkes County, where the land was too mean for profit and the markets too far away, for what little produce was produced, turning corn into liquor was the only way to turn survival into cash. A bushel of corn worth fifty cents could become ten dollars' worth of whiskey, tax-free and payable on the spot. The mountains hid the stills, the creeks cooled the mash, and the neighbours kept quiet. Legal liquor was costly and, in many 'dry' counties, still forbidden, so people drank what they trusted - what they made themselves.

Out of this rough, secret economy came legends. Junior Johnson, the farmer's son who ran liquor in a souped-up Ford, learned to outdrive the revenuers. He was eventually pardoned by Ronald Reagan and became a NASCAR hero. Willie Clay Call, from another Wilkes dynasty, kept the old art alive, turning corn, sugar and defiance into family legacy. The revenuers called it crime; the people called it liberty, and the echo of that freedom still hums in the dark woods of North Carolina.

I took a trip up into the hills of North Carolina with my old friend Rob McHale. He knows these hills well. When he hasn't driven them, he's cycled; where there's a river he's kayaked. We were looking for Tom Dooley's grave. But Rob was talking mostly about the old days of Moonshining. He'd just written and recorded a new song *'40 Ford Coupe* about the characters of these parts whose stories and spirit were woven into this landscape. We took a detour and made our way to the now legitimate Call Family Distillery.

It was late in the year: the hills burned gold and blue, the long ribs of the Brushies folding into shadow. The air was thick with pine and dust, the smell of woodsmoke drifting from somewhere unseen. Creeks flashed between the trees, and the roads twisted like something trying to shake you off. Rusted trucks slumped in the weeds; barns leaned into the dusk. It was beautiful country: hard, secretive, the kind that hides what it loves.

The distillery is a smart new shed type building but the bones of the old days lie within. We met Willie Clay Call's son, Brian, who now runs the enterprise. He showed us around, the modern vats the old stills which once were hidden in the trees and best of all his old man's cars. A big black '40 Ford Coupe, trunk still open and ready for action loading. It's the smell that takes you to another world: step inside and the air itself seems to breathe - warm, sweet, and faintly smoky. You catch the scent of mash: grain and heat, like bread rising in a wood stove. Beneath it drifts the sour tang of fermentation, sharp with yeast and apples.

Brian, affable and chilled, over a glass of Apple Pie Moonshine told us the story of his family. In the mid-1800s, a Lutheran preacher named Dan Call lived in Lynchburg, Tennessee. Alongside his ministry, he ran a small general store and - somewhat awkwardly for a man of God - operated a whiskey still on his property. Helping him was an enslaved man named Nathan 'Nearest' Green, who was an exceptional distiller and taught young Jasper 'Jack' Daniel the craft of making whiskey.

When Jack was a boy - perhaps twelve or thirteen - he was sent to work for Reverend Dan Call, who took him under his wing. According to local lore, Call introduced Jack to Green, saying:

"Uncle Nearest is the best whiskey maker I know of."

Green taught Daniel how to run a copper still, use sugar-maple charcoal to mellow the spirit - the famous Lincoln County process - and refine the art of sour mash whiskey. Jack Daniel later set up his own distillery using exactly what he had learned from *the preacher* and *the enslaved distiller*.

Years later, when the church elders confronted Reverend Call about the sin of running whiskey alongside preaching, perhaps reluctantly he chose the pulpit over the still. He sold the operation to young Jack Daniel - and the rest is Tennessee legend.

But the family tradition did not die and relocated, instead, to these hills. Its myth was written through the life of Brian's father.

They called Willie Clay Call *The Uncatchable*, a man who could drive a backroad like it was drawn on the inside of his eyelids. He ran moonshine through the ridges and hollers of Wilkes County, North Carolina, and never once got caught. As another moonshiner, Popcorn Sutton, the shaggy-bearded folk hero of North Carolina, who brewed whiskey like it was a sacrament and sold it like it was scripture said, "If you don't get caught, you ain't doin' it right."

These men weren't bootleggers in the Al Capone sense. They were rural alchemists, part outlaw, part artisan. And when they weren't running 'shine, they were tweaking their cars, adding horsepower, tuning suspension, turning their vehicles into missiles disguised as Fords and Chevys. A good moonshine car needed speed, stealth, and style. Some even had hidden compartments or smoke-release switches. Anything to lose the G-men on a twisty Appalachian road.

The process of making it was simple, brutal, beautiful. You'd find a spot deep in the woods, preferably near a stream. You'd build a fire pit and set up your copper still-most likely cobbled together from salvaged parts, oil drums, old piping, maybe even a car radiator if you were desperate. Corn mash was cooked slowly, mixed with sugar or malt, then fermented for a few days in barrels or jugs. Once ready, it was distilled in the still boiled and cooled until clear, strong spirit dripped into glass jars or stoneware jugs. The best of it came out clean, hot, and surprisingly smooth. The worst of it could blind you.

You worked at night. You kept it quiet. You trusted only a few. And you learned through trial and error - through fire and taste and patience.

It's the same way much of early America was developed. It's almost the genesis story of the nation.

I can't help thinking: isn't that the same spirit that shaped the music of the South?

Bluegrass, blues, country, gospel, rockabilly - they were all born in the same cabins and backwoods. Built on simple tools and raw ingredients. A battered guitar. A banjo with one string missing. A voice that cracked like old timber. Songs written on porches and in juke joints, passed down by ear not theory, recorded on tape recorders or never recorded at all.

Moonshine and music were made the same way: homegrown, handmade, half outlaw. Both are about transformation - taking what little you have and turning it into something powerful. Something that stings, that uplifts, that gets into your blood.

You could say the still was a kind of instrument. You could say a banjo was a kind of still. They both created something essential from raw materials: corn and water, sweat and defiance.

Moonshine is the white lightning in the bottle. Music is the lightning in the soul.

Fast forward today, and what do we find? Big corporations selling craft whiskey for $100 a bottle, made using the same techniques - and often the same recipes - that once sent men to jail. The only difference? A label. A licence. A profit margin. The same has mostly happened to the music.

Legal moonshine is just corn liquor. Real moonshine is outlawed. Made by firelight. Run by moonlight. Shared in secret. It's the difference between poetry and PR.

And still, today, it matters. It matters because the story of moonshine is the story of people who never got a fair deal, and made their own anyway. It's about not waiting for permission. Not waiting to be rescued. Not waiting for recognition. Just doing the work. Making the product. Trusting your neighbour. And mistrusting the rest.

It's not just a Southern thing. It's not even just an American thing. It's a human thing. The will to survive, to make something from nothing, to live by your wits and your craft.

That's why moonshine still glows in the national imagination. It's not just nostalgia. It's identity. It's the smell of burnt sugar and corn mash. It's the sound of tyres on gravel. It's the flicker of fire behind a shed door. It's a story passed down in whispers, and in songs.

It's a kind of truth. Spicy, strong, and maybe a little dangerous.

But then again, so is freedom.

Intermission: Moonshine Running

Way up in the backwoods, where the pines they stoop so low.
There's ghosts there in the shadows moving mighty slow.
In the gate by Tom Dooley's grave, a mobile waits to drive.
Someone took the motor out, put a Cadillac inside.

Moonshine, moonshine! Take a little drop.
Take a jug of whisky, you will find that you can't stop.

There's lightning on the sideroads, the fires lit up the sky.
All the corn's a-burning, you can't help to wonder why.
Someone's been a-snitchin', someone told the law.
Sneaky Jim, what do you think of him, creeping out the door?

Oh, me and the Bishop, and big Kev on the bass.
Heard that the revenue, had got us on their case.
So we got 'em drinking, some good ol' apple pie.
The sheriff found them singing "you gotta live before you die!"

Way down Thunder Road, burning up the sky with another load
You know we're running 'shine,
a hundred miles 'cross Wickes County Line
Fifty pounds of sugar, a hundred pounds of Rye.
When they come a-callin', where's your alibi?
Take half a cake of yeast, some water from the creek.
Say a prayer to the Lord above, we're on a winning streak.

Chapter 5: Common Ground

We had all been standing on common ground.
- Rob McHale, *Common Ground*

The first song that ever truly stopped me was *Blowin' in the Wind*. I must have been a very young boy. My mother's songs filled the kitchen and the car: safe, familiar things, songs about courting frogs, teddy bears' picnics, worms winding from the roof of a tent, when Paddy worked on the railway and swallowing a fly. But this one was different. It made me still. It made me listen.

How many roads must a man walk down? How many times? How many years?

Even then, it seemed to be asking something of me - not just to hum along, but to think, to wonder, to bear witness. It was the first time I realised that a song could map the space between us, that music could point to something greater than ourselves. It drew me into a quiet thoughtfulness a kind of private space into which I couldn't put any words.

I think I'd stumbled upon my first real taste of what I now call *common ground* - the things that make us human, that make us *us*. It's the search for the extraordinary stories of ordinary folk; the celebration of what the murdered MP Jo Cox once said in Parliament, that we are "far more united and have far more in common than that which divides us." Or the recognition, centuries earlier, in John Donne's reminder that "no man is an island, entire of itself."

Common ground isn't just a patch of shared turf. It's the recognition of what it means to be human - together. It's the quiet commitment to our shared humanity, even when it's awkward, confusing, or full of contradiction. It's standing inside the paradox of belonging - to a group, a tribe, a species - and still choosing connection. It's a kind of spiritual acknowledgment: that what unites us isn't agreement or perfection, but the courage to keep showing up for one another, again and again.

Within that space, the songwriter finds their purpose. The songwriter is the voice of the common ground - part chronicler, part critic, and sometimes the bugler for a call to arms. They gather up the fragments of who we are and turn them into songs we can recognise ourselves in. They give language to the unsaid, shape to the unspoken, and melody to the contradictions that define us. A good song doesn't divide; it reminds. It reflects both the beauty and the bruises, the laughter and the longing - the quiet courage of being human.

But where there is common ground, there is also *uncommon ground*. That's the place where we drift away from the raw and the real - where we trade truth for polish, mud for marble. It's abstracted, over-refined, arch and sanitised. It celebrates not the ordinary person but the superman and superwoman - airbrushed, remote, a reminder not of who we are, but of who we can never be.

Uncommon ground is the high-gloss mirror that reflects nothing back. It's spectacle without substance, commercialised and two-dimensional - a kind of cheap high false-art (a fart) that has lost its meaning for most folk.

And that's why the songwriter still matters. The true songwriter stands knee-deep in the mud and the glory of the common ground - listening, noticing, remembering. Their songs are stitched from the fabric of ordinary lives: the hopes, heartbreaks, and half-forgotten dreams that tell us who we really are. Against the noise of the uncommon, they keep humming the tune of belonging.

Of course, as a skinny seven-year-old, I certainly didn't see it quite like that. But the unexpected tug of those questions was in a naïve and immature way a kind of awakening. I had discovered that songs could do that!

It was the beginning for me of much that followed - the road, the songs, the long years of wandering, the search of the stories that live between people, I stumbled into the vagabond world of a songwriter and I was enchanted.

It is, in a way, an ancient role. Long before there were stages or microphones, there were people who sang the stories of their neighbours - in fields, taverns, and marketplaces. Not in the high-blown rhetoric of bards and sagas, but in the simple truth of ballads, laments and work songs. The border ballads of the North, the sea shanties, the Irish laments, the blues hollers from the Delta, the murder ballads of Appalachia - all were ways of saying: *this is who we are, this is what it feels like to be alive*.

The modern songwriter stands in that same lineage - a living witness to the ordinary miracles and heartbreaks of human life. They remind us, in words and melody, that common ground is not just something we share, but something we keep alive through the telling.

Woody Guthrie knew this. So did Dylan, Townes Van Zandt, John Prine, and Joni Mitchell. They weren't just making music; they were filing dispatches. Letters from the coalfields. Reports from motel rooms after breakups. Notes taken in diners where the coffee's weak but the stories are strong.

Not every song is political. But every good one is personal. And the personal is political, if you listen closely enough. That's why folk music - real folk, not the airbrushed, rule-bound kind - has always mattered. It doesn't sit on the fence. It chooses a side, even if that side is simply, "Let me tell you what I saw."

A good song doesn't need perfect rhymes or clever metaphors. It needs honesty. Presence. A willingness to say: this is happening, this is true. Sometimes that truth is sharp, like a protest song. Sometimes it's soft, like a lullaby for a place that's vanishing. But in every case, the songwriter is a cultural first responder. They're not theorising; they're testifying. In an age of spin, where stories come pre-packaged with agendas, that kind of unfiltered witnessing is gold.

That's why I still believe in the songwriter's role, even now, even with algorithms drowning out the subtle and celebrity culture confusing artifice for authenticity. Because somewhere, someone is writing the next dispatch from the front line. And they're probably not doing it in a penthouse. They're doing it on the edge of town.

Out in the Appalachian woods, I began to understand that calling more and more. Walking through the heat and the green, I came across the remnants of other lives - a stone chimney, a rusted car, a tiny gravestone for an infant long gone. In the Webb Brother Gas Station in Tennessee, the dirt streets of the Zuni Pueblo, the days on a Greyhound bus, marooned in a motel as the snows piled up all round - all offered up brief, fragile moments of truth.

I've also found them the among the piles of spices, cans of oil and goat meat in an old market in the Atlas Mountains, the generosity of a remote farm in the frozen lakes of Ontario, in the chaos of the crossing point from the Gambia into Senegal, but it is in the States I feel the deepest tug of all and where I first drew inspiration and still do.

I first met Rob McHale on this side of the Atlantic, when I'd booked him to appear at a festival in England. A soft-spoken North Carolinian with a wry smile, he returned the favour a year later, inviting me to his home patch for a series of gigs and a crash course in the heartland of small-town America.

We played libraries and coffee bars, churches and listening rooms. Davidson, Walkertown, Kannapolis. Places that don't make the news but are full of people still hungry for stories, still willing to sit and really *listen*. Rob is a songwriting chronicler in the best sense: he's lived a life and looks at the world through his own particular spectacles. Before music, he flew mail planes - the sort that look held together with prayer and chewing gum. He's farmed a bit, bred horses. That sense of steadiness and purpose runs through his songs. Nothing flashy. Just lines that land exactly where they need to.

Rob writes brilliant and rare songs about characters from history, female pirates who stalked the Carolina coast, the ghost of Jesse James, the strange tale of Tom Dooley, but I think it is the small town, local songs I love the best. The ones about the quiet, intimate moments, sitting in a park, playing a gig in a coffee shop, the mining of local mountain. His signature piece, in my view, is *Julia's Tally House* - a song about a small diner in Troutman that served fried chicken, meatloaf, and community. Rob and a friend sit on the porch, realising they no longer recognise the faces going past. It's about more than gentrification. It's about disconnection. The slow fade of familiarity. A place you love turning into somewhere you merely live.

That song could be about anywhere - a pub in Derbyshire, a bar in Montana - and that's the point. It *is* about everywhere. It's a local dispatch with universal truth.

Staying with Rob felt like stepping inside one of his songs. His house backed onto Lake Norman, quiet as a prayer. I spent long mornings on the deck with a borrowed Martin guitar, letting old songs find their way back to my fingers. Rob made coffee with attention of a watchmaker. We'd sit and talk gigs, audiences, stories. His mind never stops working - not in a frantic way, but in the steady rhythm of someone who knows the value of the next line.

He's not chasing fame. He's recording the world around him. One song, one line, one front porch at a time.

His song *Common Ground* begins in Boston, walking with doctors and sailors, nuns and bums - ordinary people who meet, however briefly, at the same level. It ends with the simplest revelation: *we had all been standing on common ground.* It captures something I've spent a lifetime trying to describe - that fragile, miraculous moment when music dissolves the distances between us.

If Rob is the careful observer, David Childers is the proclaimer. We met in Kannapolis - an old mill town now redefining itself, like so many others. We were sharing a bill in a room filled with that rare and beautiful thing: silence that means attention.

David arrived with a guitar that looked like it had been in a bar fight and won. He sat down, opened his mouth, and it was as if the walls leaned in. His voice is part gravel, part gospel. His presence, pure magnetism. His songs don't meander; they *declare* with the authority of someone who's seen what he's singing about.

David's from Mount Holly - lawyer by trade, poet by instinct, painter by temperament. He knows the power of words but never wastes them. His lyrics range from spiritual wrestling matches to working-class portraits drawn with a coal miner's hand. In songs like *Cold Steel Arms* (of the factory town) and *Quiet In the House of The Rising Sun*.

He's there to *tell you something true*. If that's entertainment, fine. If not, also fine. What I admired most was his clarity. He doesn't dress things up or turn a phrase for cleverness. He writes like someone who has seen what happens when people don't tell the truth - and refuses to be part of that silence.

In that way, David is an old-time preacher man - the kind who stands in the middle of the storm and shouts so the people in the back can hear. Between Rob's porchlight and David's lightning, you glimpse the two poles of American song: tenderness and outrage, truth whispered insistently and proclaimed. Both are needed. Both are true. Both, in their way, hold open that patch of shared earth we call common ground.

The thing is about songwriters like this, and the better-known ones, is they *keep on keeping on*. Mostly you don't get fortunes or much fame doing this. You don't get too old or out of fashion. Because you were never in fashion and you were always too old or not pretty enough. You do what you because you have no idea of how not to.

A few years ago in Asheville, I saw Eric Andersen perform - one of the last survivors of the old Greenwich Village tribe, conscious of the blood that flows through the city and the streets they walk through. He shuffled on stage in dark jeans and a black trilby, a sheaf of papers on a music stand, his voice a little worn but still fierce. Between songs he muttered fragments, half-apologies, half-poems. The room was quiet, reverent.

Looking at him, I thought of the line from Ricky Nelson: *If memories were all I sang, I'd rather drive a truck*. But Andersen wasn't purely peddling nostalgia. He was still chasing the song. Still keeping on. The voice cracked, the phrasing imperfect - but the commitment undimmed. It struck me that this is what it means to be a witness: to keep singing even when your voice falters, because the truth still needs to be told.

Travelling westward through Appalachia, across the graveyards of Proctor and into the red deserts of New Mexico, I have started to think of songs as the modern trail markers of the human spirit. Each one tells us where someone has been, what they found, and how they survived. The songwriter walks that line between personal confession and public truth - between solitude and solidarity.

From Dylan's questions, in the brilliant honesty of John Prine, the rueful reflection of Guy Clark, in the raw truth of Joni Mitchell from the lost commons of England to the backroads of the Carolinas, I've come to see that the true work of the songwriter isn't to divide or to dazzle, but to remind. To bear witness. To make us look again at each other and say: yes, this is happening; yes, this is true.

In July 2003, just a few months after the death of his beloved June Carter and a few months before his own, Johnny Cash gave his final live performance. Not at Madison Square Garden. Not at the Grand Ole Opry. But at a small wooden stage at the foot of the Clinch Mountains in Virginia - at the Carter Family Fold.

The Fold is a music venue built on the original Carter family homestead, not far from Maces Spring, where A.P., Sara, and Maybelle Carter had lived and sung and created what we now think of as country music. The Carters didn't invent the field song, but they gathered it, recorded it, shaped it. They took the ballads of the mountains and gave them a new kind of permanence.

And there, in that humble space with folding chairs and plywood walls, Johnny Cash - frail, grieving, hunched over a microphone - sang one last time.

There's a black-and-white video of it. He's seated throughout, with a glass of water nearby, oxygen not far away. He barely raises his voice. But it's all there: the weight, the history, the love.

He speaks more than he sings. He tells the crowd he's doing this in memory of June. He stumbles. He shakes. He smiles. And then, when he finally sings *Ring of Fire*, it's not defiance anymore. It's surrender. It's a man returning to the seam that sustained him - the place, the people, the porch where the music began.

Cash didn't go out in a blaze of glory. He went out with a dispatch. One last report from the front line - from the hollers and hymns of a country that never quite let go of him, even when it tried.

Maybe all these songs are really one long conversation, a chain of dispatches about what it means to be alive together. We can't own common ground. We can only stand on it, briefly, listening.

And somewhere, still, the wind is asking how many roads it will take.

Chapter 6: A Bridge Across the River

On a sunny Sunday morn,
On a bridge across the river,
The scent of weed was in the air.
We were called on to deliver.

That's how the song begins.

I wrote it the morning after my debut in Music City. The night before, I had stood - somewhat shakily - on a stage at a songwriter's circle, surrounded by Grammy-winners, rising stars, and men and women with voices soaked in heartbreak and honey. I was the outsider, the interloper with a guitar and a handful of songs. But somehow, there I was.

It's said that Nashville first earned the name *Music City* not from the Grand Ole Opry, or the studios of Music Row, or even the rough-edged bars of Lower Broadway, but from a queen, an ocean away.

In the 1870s, a group of young singers from Fisk University - freed slaves and the children of slaves - set out from Nashville on a mission to keep their college alive. They called themselves the Fisk Jubilee Singers. With little more than courage, harmony, and a horse-drawn wagon, they toured the length and breadth of America and then crossed the Atlantic to sing before the crowned heads of Europe.

When they reached England, they performed for Queen Victoria herself. The story goes that she sat utterly still as those voices - raw, pure, filled with sorrow and hope - rose in the great hall. When the final note faded, she is said to have turned to an attendant and declared, "With such beautiful voices, they must come from a Music City."

It may be folklore - nobody knows her exact words - but the title stuck. Nashville was christened *Music City* not by a marketing man or record executive, but by the sound of its own people, carried across oceans. The name came not from fame, but from spirit - from a choir born in hardship who sang the songs of their ancestors and, in doing so, gave a whole city its soul.

That morning, still buzzing and bewildered, I went walking.

Down Broadway, through a Nashville not yet fully awake.

The bars were shuttered, for now. The streets sticky from last night's spilled beer and spilled dreams. Soon enough the place would come alive, bands slugging it out for attention over the whoops of tourists drinking Bud Light from plastic glasses. But in that moment, as I sat on the sidewalk just off Broadway sipping a coffee, it was just me, the ghosts, and a faint breeze drifting up from the Cumberland River.

The Cumberland River, a crossing place. where ferrymen once rowed wagons and travellers from one bank to the other. You can still feel them somehow - those patient figures waiting in the half-light, steadying their boats while the river slides by, brown and slow, whispering of where it's been and where it's going.

Later, this river brought the great steamboats up from New Orleans - floating casinos, brothels, concert halls, where wild and unleashed people drank, danced, made and lost fortunes and slept with the willing and the paid for. It was a heaving artery of sound and sin, threading the land together. Immigrants and chancers, thieves and believers, bringing fiddles and folk tunes that fused with African rhythms and gospel hollers, all of it stewing into something rich and unruly.

But the chugging belching river boats brought something else: slaves.

The heart of Nashville's slave-trading business was not far from where I sat. On the corner of Fourth and Charlotte, in the 1840s and the 1850s, there were a series of slave trading businesses there, with names that sounded like accountants such as Glover & Boyd, Dabbs & Porter, James & Harrison, Lyles & Hitchings, and others. These genteel-sounding enterprises sold men, women, and children. Nashville was not just complicit in slavery - it profited from it.

Nashville, I thought not for the first time, is a place where opposites meet. Even in its beginnings. It's a place for the Ferryman. We need the ferryman because we live in a world of opposites - sin and grace, despair and redemption - and someone must hold the rope between them. The ferryman is what we need when who we are lives on both sides of the river.

During the Civil War it was a city torn in half - a Confederate capital that fell almost without a fight. Tennessee had voted to secede, but Nashville never quite believed it. Its merchants traded north, its hills hid Union sympathisers, and when the bluecoats marched in across the Cumberland in 1862, the city surrendered rather than burn.

For the rest of the war, it lived in uneasy occupation - rebel and loyalist sharing the same streets, soldiers and freedmen and preachers and gamblers all crowded together in a swirl of suspicion and necessity. It was neither North nor South, not conquered but not free, a place of divided hearts and uneasy grace.

Maybe that's where the pattern was set. Ever since, Nashville has seemed to live at the crossing point - between sin and salvation, rebellion and redemption. Its songs are born from that tension, that strange harmony of contradiction.

Even today, when you walk its streets, you might sense the paradox and contradiction, the echo of bugles over the river, the whisper of hymns rising from the broken ground. It's a city forever standing in the doorway, half in the dark, half in the light.

He cried, "You all deceived yourselves!"
And the drummers played a roll.
Let the dark-haired girl in leather pants
Sanctify... sanctify my soul.

Finishing my reverie and my coffee, I found myself drawn to the Johnny Cash Museum. It felt like the right place to go - the shrine of the man who, more than any other, carried the sound of that divided heart. If anyone might be a Ferryman, it would be Johnny Cash.

Behind the glass, you can see the life of a man who was tossed around by his inner contradictions: the guitar he played at Folsom Prison, its varnish worn pale where his thumb struck it raw; a tattered set list scrawled on hotel stationery; the Bible he carried on the road, pages soft from use; a telegram from June, folded and refolded until the creases turned to scars.

You move through rooms of darkness and light - stage lights, prison bars, grainy footage of him singing *I Got Stripes* to a hall full of convicts, the sound raw and defiant. Then the photographs: the young soldier, the father, the hollow-eyed prophet recording *Hurt* at the end.

He was never just the "Man in Black." He was the man in grey. And that's why we trust him. Because he wasn't selling perfection. He was testifying to pain, guilt, regret - and hope. Cash sang for the broken, but he never pretended not to be broken himself. That's why prisoners believed him when he sang at Folsom, and Presidents listened when he sang of America's wounded heart. He stood at the crossroads between gospel and murder ballad, hymnal and honky-tonk, and somehow held them both together.

Cash was never just a singer. He was a man forever crossing rivers - between sin and salvation, fame and ruin, rebellion and grace. He sang for prisoners and Presidents, carried gospel to the jails and guilt to the church pews. If Elvis was the spark, Cash was the smoke - drifting through every contradiction America ever produced. Back in the last chapter, I thought of him as one of the great correspondents of America's struggle, writing bulletins in verse and chord. Here, he was something different again: almost a patron saint of the city, his shadow stitched into every stage, every lyric sheet, every dream of redemption that still drifts up and down Broadway.

Looking at that old Martin guitar, I thought of the ferryman again. Cash spent his life on that boat, rowing back and forth between heaven and hell, carrying the rest of us across with him. He sang the darkness, but he didn't stay there. He sang the light, but he knew its price.

Who wants to try for heaven?
Who's heading down to hell?
You've a chance to repent your crimes
At the tolling of the bell...

Emerging into the sunny daylight out of the museum, I found the city had sprung to life. The Tennessee Titans were playing the Kansas City Chiefs across the river at the Nissan Stadium The atmosphere was festive and amiable and thousands of cheerful fans for both teams were heading down Broadway to cross the river via the John Seigenthaler Pedestrian Bridge.

With nothing better to do I tagged along with them. Not to go to the game, just to be in the congregation.

The bridge was broad and graceful and the river below timeless. Football fans in Titans jerseys ambled toward the stadium. No one was hurrying or fussing much. Some walked in twos and threes laughing and slapping each other on the back, some stood in convivial silence looking at the slow, flow of the river; little groups were singing, others walked on, balancing toddlers on shoulders and beers in hands. A drummer banged a rhythm on a snare. A girl in tight leather pants danced like she was conjuring spirits.

There, I saw him. A preacher, arms raised, feet astride, voice ringing out through a crackling speaker:

“If you wanna appreciate the cure,” he hollered, “you’ve got… gotta know the sin.”

I had to smile; it seemed to sum Nashville up. Don’t look for redemption until you’ve sampled the opposite. Redemption is a beautiful idea. But it only has meaning if you know what you’re trying to be redeemed from.

Redemption a big deal down here in the South. Actually, the idea of redemption and reinvention runs through much of the myth of the USA. You keep running across it - a sense that you aren’t stuck with who you’ve been. You can be saved. Awkward, corny, though it may be.

And at the heart of the redemption is the idea you might reinvent yourself as someone better. It is why so many people left miserable lives all over the world and went to those shores. Don’t we love this story? It is the precious spring of hope.

In America, outlaws can become lawmen, as much as lawmen can fall from grace and become outlaws. It depends upon the choices you make.

Tomorrow's not a promise,
The good Lord does insist...
You refuse to change your ways,
You're on... old Satan's list.

The belief that you're not stuck with who you were. That sin doesn't have the final word. That you can change your tune - mid-song - and people might just sing along.

Captain Tom Ryman, towards the end of 19th-century, owner of 37 riverboats and profiting from the steamy, seedy and salacious world that followed his boats everywhere, was drawn to hear the Rev Sam Jones preach in Nashville. He was checking out the opposition, for the good preacher had railed against the corrupt and sinful goings-on on the boats from which the captain prospered. Ryman was so affected by the passionate rhetoric of Jones that he, there and then, committed to building a place where such words of God could be better heard. This was opened in 1892 as the Union Gospel Tabernacle which was renamed the Ryman Auditorium upon the captain's death. From here was launched the Grand Ole Opry, a weekly radio show which has run since 1925. It's the mother church of country music.

I once found myself at the Ryman Auditorium back up the road behind me, the spiritual home of country music. The old brick building, showing its genesis as a Baptist church with a semicircle of polished wooden pews, was full. Inside, the mood was reverent, if quietly unsettled. Only the day before, in Las

Vegas, a madman had opened fire on a crowd at a music festival.

There were no announcements. No dedications. No speeches.

But Alison Krauss came on stage, and she sang.

The hush in the room before that first note was like nothing I'd ever known. A thousand people breathing as one, waiting. The pews creaked as people leaned forward, instinctively, as if the very building were preparing to listen. Then the fiddle raised, the bow touched the strings, and her voice unfurled.

From the first note, it was clear: this was not the rhinestone version of America, sugarised and sentimentalised. This was the real deal. Her voice, her band, and the songs - they were rooted deep. Songs whose veins ran back into the soil of the country itself. Songs like *Down to the River to Pray*, said to be an African-American spiritual, an Appalachian hymn, a gospel cry - all at once.

In the band was Sidney Cox, braces straining over his belly, steel guitar gleaming on his lap, looking like he'd just stepped off a Tennessee porch. Or climbed down from the pulpit. There was truth in the music - simple, luminous, deeply human. No big show. Just soul.

When she sang *I Am Weary, Let Me Rest*, I found myself thinking of the grave markers I had found in Appalachian Hills. A young mother. An unnamed child. The song floated above the pews like a hymn for everyone who's carried something heavy too long.

And as the final notes lingered, I heard again that echo from the bridge.

"If you wanna appreciate the cure, you gotta know the sin."

The memories of that evening made me thirsty for some more moonshine music. So, I went looking.

Broadway was by now wall-to-wall noise. Band after band playing soft rock with a remarkable lack of subtlety on little stages in crowded bars, trading authenticity for volume. Tourists crowded the streets with beer-fuelled inane grins wearing plastic cowboy hats and brand-new plaid and checked shirts. The heat grew and between the odd beer or two myself, a burger and a half decent taco, I grimly kept up my search.

It felt like Nashville had become a parody of itself.

I'd almost given up. But as I passed a small bar called Layla's, something stopped me. A rough honky-tonk rhythm, pure and true, bleeding out the door. I ducked in for a beer and found the Eskimo Brothers.

Ferrymen.

Redemption.

They were everything that had been missing all day.

There they were: David Graham on guitar, a Fonz-meets-Springsteen figure with a battered Telecaster, grinning as he made that thing sing. The stand-up bassist, Jim, was a Jim Carrey lookalike doing comedy with his face and acrobatics with his bass. The drummer, bearded and bespectacled, was all business, keeping it tight while the others ran wild.

They tore through a rockabilly version of *Fat Bottomed Girls*, then threw down *Folsom Prison Blues* like a runaway freight train. Their originals were glorious roughnecks of songs - about cars, horses, fights, and freedom.

Then, David paused. “We don’t get paid except by you,” he said, resting his guitar on one arm. “If you like us, show us. And don’t forget the girls behind the bar - they ain’t paid either!”

Jim hopped down with an ice bucket. It came back overflowing. Tens, twenties, applause.

And on they went: Ernest Tubb, Hank Williams, a roadhouse version of *Suspicious Minds*. People danced. Couples smiled. A seventy-year-old man jived in braces. For a moment, it was all real again.

This was the Nashville I’d hoped for.

The next day, I headed out of town.

But something of the place stayed with me. Not just the twang of Telecasters or the sight of hopeful songwriters passing around lyric sheets in back bars. Not just the ghosts of slaves and gamblers, of Confederate flags and church choirs.

It was the feeling that your story isn't finished yet. That whoever you are, you might still have a verse to add. The memory of that morning on the bridge, watching the preacher shout, the drummer pound, and the leather-clad girl spin. And for a moment, I believed.

Hey, Lord! Set us free!
Hey, my Lord! Set us free!

In redemption.

In reinvention.

In the truth hidden in contradiction.

Not perfect. Not pure. But real.

And sometimes, that's more than enough.

Nashville is the birthplace of Goo Goo Clusters and the home of Gibson Guitars. But more than that, it's the city where contradictions dance together in time.

Intermission:
On A Bridge Across The River

On a sunny Sunday morn, on a bridge across the river,
The scent of weed was in the air, we were called on to deliver
By a preacher who was calling out To let the good Lord in:
"If you wanna appreciate the cure,
You've got.... gotta know the sin."

Good news is hard to come by, so let me give it to ya.
The football fans just passed him by,
        though some said "Hallelujah!"
The kids, they rode on shoulders of the Titans and the lame.
The young men, they just hollered out,
To lose... would be a shame.

Who wants to try for heaven? Who's heading down to hell?
You've a chance to repent your crimes at the tolling of the bell.
Tomorrow's not a promise, the good Lord does insist.
You refuse to change your ways,
You're on... old Satan's list.

One lonely soul stopped to pass the time
with the preacher and the thief
Most others sang and drank their beer,
with the Kansas City Chiefs
He cried, "You all deceived yourselves!"
and the drummers played a roll
Let the dark-haired girl in leather pants
Sanctify… sanctify my soul.

There the spirit of the river boats,
that swam up from the sea
And the Captain cried, "This journey's done,
won't you tie me to a tree?"
And the girls who knew a thing or two,
sang, "That ain't how it's gonna be."
Hey, Lord! Set us free!
Hey, my Lord! Set us free!

Listen online: arcr.uk/gtlfamusic

Chapter 7: Ladders to the Sky

The sheer size of America hides things. Its strangeness gets overlooked, folded into the endless miles. Whole peoples disappear into the landscape, their stories swallowed by rivers and ridges, by the noise of progress.

In the hollows of Appalachia, there are families who say their blood runs back to a time before the settlers came - the Melungeons, people of uncertain origin and dark complexion, half-remembered in rumour and song. Some say they were Portuguese, some African, some the scattered remnant of a lost tribe of Israel. Others think they were simply the first to be forgotten - descendants of wanderers who found their way into the mountains long before Columbus came ashore.

Most of us came here on ships - Europeans, Africans, all of us newcomers blown across the ocean by need or by hope. Others came earlier, when the world was young, crossing the land bridge from the north as ice still gripped the earth. Some may have wandered from the south, moving slowly up through forest and desert, following the rivers and the deer.

So, who were the first Americans? Is that even a reasonable question?

It can be an important one as for many people, being first seems to grant automatic rights, possession or ownership.

Consider the truculent ten-year-old who clings fiercely to a deflated football found in the garden. When asked to share or let someone else have it, he protests, "But I had it first. It's mine." Claiming to be the first gives you the right to reject all newcomers to the opportunity.

However, another principle often emerges in history. The owner of the biggest club or stick believes this grants them rights to the deflated football and everything else. This principle often trumps 'firstness'. "I have a bigger stick, so it is mine," they might say.

Then, a not-so-subtle sleight-of-hand occurs. The one with the bigger stick no longer claims possession is a direct result of their having a bigger stick. Instead, they claim it's actually because "we were the first after all." And so, the deflated football and the rest of the world is actually theirs.

Who were the first? It was not the British, the Spanish, or even the 'Native Americans'. Perhaps it was the Pueblo people still found in New Mexico and Arizona. They claim an ancestry of thousands and thousands of years.

I had stumbled over the existence of the Pablo people by accident, almost spotting them in the corner of my eye as I read and explored books on the Internet about the Old West. Shamefully, in my ignorance I thought at first, they were Mexican people, the northern outliers of the old Spanish empire down in Mexico. But then I came across drawings and photographs of ancient buildings, strange, beautiful structures, mysterious, with windows but no doors. They were shaped like a curved cube seemingly built of the earth on which they stood with entry through the roof and via a ladder.

These structures resembled the shells of enormous, ancient, earth-made turtles. I imagined that, like a turtle retracting into its shell when threatened, the inhabitants could pull up their ladders during times of danger and remain safe inside their smoky, secure homes.

This unique aspect of their culture piqued my curiosity and led me to learn more. I realised that these people were neither Mexicans, Aztec migrating from the south, 'Native Americans' or yet another 'lost tribe of Israel'. They were a distinct group with mysterious origins, predating other civilizations that claimed primacy in this region.

I had to learn more. I discovered the existence of the Zuni Pueblo. They live on a reservation of about twelve square miles and there about 6,000 of them. Their pueblo stands on the red edge of New Mexico, older than any colony, older than the rise of the Aztec or the first prayer whispered in English on this continent. Their language, *Shiwi'ma*, has no relatives - a linguistic orphan, as if it had grown from the stone itself. To speak it is to breathe something untranslatable, a voice from before history began keeping score.

I had to go. And made plans based on a road trip I was making around the New Mexico.

There were no hotels or guest houses in the reservation and no campsite. It seemed a private place, a place anxious not to be invaded. There were instructions about not taking photographs without permission. Via the internet, I made contact with Tom, who seemed to be some sort of liaison person. His reply was warm and welcoming. He confirmed there was no accommodation but suggested an RV Campsite a few miles away, and, giving me his mobile number, told me to make contact with him when I got there.

Somewhere near Gallup, Route 66 gave up and turned into the Interstate. Our road peeled off into quieter territory, and we drove for more than an hour without seeing another soul. Then came a sign, weathered and almost apologetic: Welcome to the Zuni Pueblo.

We got lost looking for our RV park. A GPS failure landed us in the wrong place, so we asked an elderly man walking along the road for directions. He turned, smiled, and spoke with such warmth that I felt I'd just received a sacred blessing rather than simple directions. "Another fourteen miles," he said. I laughed to myself: *You certainly are Native American. Possibly never home.*

We found the El Morro RV Park just as the sun began to fall. It curled into the hills near a place called the Ancient Ways Café, which was closed for the evening. We parked and settled in. The next morning, I wandered over to the café for breakfast. I bumped into an older man with long grey hair tied in a ponytail and a neatly clipped beard. His name was Red Wolf. His paintings hung on the walls of the café and a hand-lettered notice outside offered his services for spiritual readings.

The café had a curious atmosphere - a blend of Navajo, Mexican, and the leftover parts of the 1960s. Kindness hummed through it like background music. Signs on the walls read: *We serve everyone here*. Another: *Be the person your dog thinks you are*. I had a lazy breakfast, full of coffee and quiet joy, and learned of an open mic night planned across the road. The woman behind the counter, Monica, beamed when I asked if I could play.

So, when people call Zuni the oldest continuously inhabited settlement in the United States, the phrase feels almost absurd.

The Zuni are not the beginning of America - they are what came *before* America, the deep root of the continent's memory.

To walk there is to feel the ground remembering. The wind carries a kind of knowing. And as I came down that long, straight road and the first low houses appeared against the pale horizon, I thought how much depends on where you start. For some, America begins at Plymouth Rock or Jamestown, or with a flag raised on a battlefield. But for others - for the Zuni - it began in the dark world below, with the first ladder into the sky.

I thought of all the roads that had led here: the ancient paths from the canyon, the Spanish trails, the wagon ruts, Route 66 itself. Every one of them seemed to end in this stillness. After so many miles of motion, the feeling was almost vertiginous. Finding America, I realised, depends on where you start. For me, that afternoon, it began here - among ladders, dust, and silence - in a place that had never needed discovering.

The buildings reminded me of rural Morocco - dust -coloured adobe, sun-bleached wood, a single paved road threading through a landscape of grit and silence.

We returned to Zuni that day, this time aiming for the visitor centre. On the drive, I found myself reflecting on a phrase I often use: the simple, mysterious ricochets of chance. A detour, a conversation, a wrong turn - these were the ingredients of discovery. Why did this place already feel like it meant something to me? I was hovering above the surface of something deeper, unable yet to explain its pull.

Zuni. I had a sense we were approaching something unusual, something older and more layered than the paved road we had followed. But when we drove into town, my companion sighed in disappointment. This wasn't what she'd hoped for: scattered bungalow-style buildings, stray dogs, a few shops selling traditional jewellery. She wanted it to feel more "authentic." I understood the feeling, but I couldn't share it. To me, this was authentic - people living their culture in the twenty-first century, not staged, not frozen in time. Just real.

Zuni Pueblo is unlike other Native American reservations. It has been continuously inhabited for longer than almost any place in North America. Archaeologists trace Puebloan culture back at least two thousand years, and the Zuni claim a lineage that stretches much further - seven thousand years or more. Some, like our later guide Kenny, speak of fifty thousand years. This isn't a people who were merely displaced by colonisers; they were already ancient by the time the Spanish arrived.

At the centre, we met Tom - a soft-spoken man in a loose ponytail and no particular rush. Zuni time, like Zuni space, moves differently. He called Kenny, their head guide, who was also an archaeologist, a shaman, a tribal elder, and, that day, a tyre repairman. He held down multiple roles. He arrived in oily jeans and a sleeveless top and offered us a twenty-minute crash course in the Zuni world.

The Zuni, or *A:shiwi* people, are a distinct linguistic and cultural group within the Puebloan family. Their language is a linguistic isolate, unrelated to any other in the world. That uniqueness, perhaps, reflects their worldview: a deeply interwoven cosmology in which spirit, place, and purpose are indivisible.

Kenny told us about the Four Worlds. We sat on a low wall outside the centre, the sun casting long shadows across the dusty square.

"So how long have your people been here?" I asked.

He rubbed a hand across his chin. "The scientists say maybe twelve, eighteen thousand years. We say longer. Much longer. Maybe fifty thousand. But time doesn't work the same way for us. It's not just history. It's memory." Archaeology can point back a couple of millennia; oral tradition spirals back further still. But maybe that's the point: the story isn't a straight line. It's a web, a puzzle, a ladder rising through worlds.

According to the Zuni, they did not come across the land bridge from the north, nor drift up from the south. They came from *below* - climbing ladders from the underworld through the mouth of the Grand Canyon into the world of light. It's a story both literal and symbolic, a creation told in geography. The Zuni say they did not conquer this world but emerged into it by invitation - the earth allowing them to surface, to live in balance with what was already here.

As Kenny explained. "The world we live in now? It's the fourth one. We came from below - from three other worlds that were destroyed, changed, or left behind. We were half-formed back then. Web-footed, they say. But we climbed ladders, up from darkness. Each time we rose, we learned more. We became more human."

"Ladders?" I asked. "Actual ladders?"

He smiled. "Yes. Symbolic and real. Made of wood. Made of prayer. You climb, or you don't. Depends on who you are."

He paused, then continued.

"When we came into this world, into a place now called the Grand Canyon, the All-Father gave us the Heart of Mother Earth to protect. We were told to carry it and bury it in the Middle Place and that we had to find that place. We split into two groups. Some stayed behind to guard it. The rest of us went wandering to find where it should be buried. It was a long, long journey. Some of us would stop and give up and those became the other Pueblos but some of us kept going till we got here through a great circular route to the place we had started from."

I listened as he spoke, sensing that this wasn't just mythology. It was geography, psychology, spirituality - all rolled into a lived landscape.

"And so, you found it eventually?"

Kenny nodded. "Yes. Our people met again. The guardians and the wanderers. They buried the Heart here, in what is now the Middle Village of Zuni."

"Still here?"

"Sure, would you like to see it?"

How often in your life do you get to see the genesis stone?

The place itself was almost nothing: a square of dirt, a wooden ladder leaning toward the roof of a humble house, another ladder pointing into the sky. Yet it was, for Kenny, the centre of the world. "This is where the dances happen," he said, lowering his voice instinctively. "Not for tourists. Not for photos. For the spirits, and the ancestors, and for balance."

He spoke of the dances as relationship rather than performance - each step meaning something, each movement calling something into being. In Zuni practice, the physical and the spiritual are not separate. The dancers become embodiments of sacred beings who help maintain harmony between the worlds.

"You have to live in harmony with all things," Kenny said. "The land, the spirits, the ancestors, even your enemies. Harmony is not peace exactly - it's balance."

As he spoke, I understood more clearly how Zuni belief was not just religion, but a way of ordering the universe - a cosmology that mapped not only time and space but behaviour and responsibility.

Later he pointed across the valley to a flat-topped rise. "When the floods came, the people climbed up there. But the waters didn't stop. So, the chief made a sacrifice - his son and daughter. He gave them to the water to save everyone else. They turned to stone. Their footprints still lead up the mountain - right into the sky."

That evening, as the light drained out of the sky, I thought about how his stories carried weight but also lightness. The Zuni weren't frozen in their myths - they lived with them. Myth wasn't separate from the dust under our boots or the adobe walls around us. It was folded into everything. Time breathes in and out.

But then the people with the bigger stick came. In the centre of Zuni stands a crumbling adobe mission church, built by Franciscan missionaries in the early 1600s. The church is abandoned now; roof gone, authority disclaimed. Now the Catholic Church has gifted it to the village. The village don't want it. Basically poor, making a living from craft and artwork such a pottery, silver work and fetishes, paying for the upkeep of a building established by an alien culture is beyond them. (A Zuni fetish is a small carved figure, often of an animal, believed to hold spiritual power and embody traits like protection, healing, or renewal.)

It is the monument of a collision - not just of empires, but of worlds. Colonisation here was not merely physical; it was spiritual, a rupture in the rhythm of belief. In 1680, the Pueblo peoples rose in revolt, driving the Spanish out for twelve years, burning churches and reclaiming ancestral ways. At Zuni, the mission was torched, its roof destroyed.

What remains is not a place of worship, but a quiet ruin - a symbol of time's layered flow, where memory and resistance still echo in the dust.

The next morning Tom had arranged for me to meet Eileen Yatsattie, a traditional Zuni potter whose quiet dedication embodied so much of what Kenny had been telling us. Eileen began making pottery in 1973 at the age of thirteen, learning from her grandmother, Margaret Walela, and her great-grandmother, Catalina Zunie. Her workspace was small, plain, and full of patience.

She still collected and processed her own clay, pigments, and plants, as she was taught by Josephine Nahohai, an elder potter. Every tool seemed imbued with purpose. Her hands moved slowly, carefully, with the kind of authority that only comes from repetition over decades, rolling the clay into coils, smoothing it by hand, then coating it with a fine slip before burnishing it to a quiet glow. On mine a small frog clings to the side - a symbol of rain and renewal - while across the surface runs a pattern of careful geometric lines, like the measured breath of the desert itself. On one face, a deer is painted with its mouth open and an arrow running to its heart: the Zuni heart-line, showing the breath of life, the spirit moving within. It feels less like decoration and more like a conversation - between the seen and unseen, between clay, rain, and the pulse of the world.

I asked if she felt she was making something old or something new. She smoothed a curve on the side of a vessel with her thumb and answered, "Both. Everything I make is old, because it comes from a memory that's older than me. But it's also new, because I've touched it. It has my story now too."

Clay, paint, and fire: the most ordinary of materials. Yet in her hands they became myth, shaped and burnished into vessels that seemed to whisper their own histories. She spoke of clay as sacred, fire as transformation. Watching her work, I felt that the Zuni stories weren't something preserved in museums. They were alive, being made and remade with every bowl, every brushstroke.

Back in England, I showed the pot to my friend, Phil the Potter, a maker of beautiful, almost timeless work himself. He admired the craftsmanship, the process of coiling the clay, then covering it with a slip, and then polishing it to an almost perfect surface, the placing on it, of the symbolic and representational.

An intriguing part of his own approach is looking at the overlooked artefacts of ancient times, the bricks, the plasters, the discarded shards of pottery, and then letting that spark his own work. Some of his more recent work reflects this, not just in the shape, but the texture itself. His recent pieces have an incredible tactile quality, the glaze gritty and rough as if rolled into the sands of time. He has even taken broken fragments of pottery hundreds of years old and worked them into new pieces, like Eileen bottling timelessness in a piece of clay.

Art is the weft in the warp of time, he mused, looking at the strange symbols on Eileen's work, a moment of immortality captured in the flow.

When I look at it now, I hear again Kenny's phrase about ladders to the sky, and Eileen's quiet insistence that every vessel she made was both old and new. Elaine's pot feels the same: old in the memory it carries, new in the touch that gave it form.

In Zuni, myth and memory folded into every stone, every bowl, every step of a dance.

I had arrived in Zuni with the common myth still in my bones: America as a fresh chapter, a frontier waiting to be tamed. But that collapsed like sunbaked clay. This was not a new world. This was a world older than most - older than Columbus's ships, older than Bible-belt revival tents, older than cattle trails and railroads. A world whose people had charted the migration of spirit and landscape before there was even the faintest idea of "America."

And the Zuni were first?

Before the pueblos of the desert, there were cities of earth. Along the great rivers of the East and South, the Mississippian people raised temples of soil and sky - vast mounds shaped by hand, tier upon tier, each one a prayer pressed into the land. From Cahokia to Etowah, they built plazas wide as dreams, traded copper from the Great Lakes for shells from the Gulf, and lived by the rhythm of flood and harvest.

And then, almost as quietly as they had risen, they were gone. The mounds stood, but the fires went out. Drought, flood, the long shadows of hunger and unrest - and later, the invisible storms of disease carried on strange winds - thinned the great towns until only the grass remained. But the people did not vanish. They became the ancestors of the Choctaw and Chickasaw, the Creek and the Natchez, still carrying songs and symbols older than any map.

Their earthworks endure - soft green hills in fields and forests - reminders that America did not begin with discovery or arrival, but with many emergences. The land was already speaking in a thousand tongues before history learned to listen.

So, in the end who were the first Americans? Is time really that linear? Maybe there is physical time - the great cosmic metronome ticking since the Big Bang, the light of distant stars carrying us news from millions of years ago. In that sense, we are always peering backward, our gaze slipping through the deep corridors of before. The astronomer looks through a telescope and sees not what is but what was - the ghost of a star still burning its way toward us. But human time is different. It is not a straight line but a story, looping, echoing, returning. When we speak of beginnings, they are artefacts of the tale - arbitrary but charged with meaning.

The Zuni seem to understand this instinctively. Their stories do not begin with conquest or discovery, but with emergence - people climbing from one world into another. The past is not gone but layered beneath your feet; the ancestors are still here, just one level down. Maybe that's why this place feels so still. You sense that time has not vanished, only folded - that that every sound and gesture is happening in more than one age at once.

As I have said elsewhere, it's not 'once upon a time' but twice, three, four, many upon a time. Each telling summons the world anew. The start of America, then, is not a date or a document, but the moment a people decided to call their story into being - to walk out from the dark and climb a ladder into the light.

Chapter 8:
Billy the Kid and the Fallen Angel

Paula Angel is not a name you'll find in the guidebooks. Even in Las Vegas, New Mexico, she is barely remembered. A footnote, if that. No plaques, no ballads sung in the plaza. Her story lies half-buried in a handful of newspaper clippings and a few scattered mentions in dusty histories. Not a legend, not a folk heroine - just a young woman whose death was quickly swallowed by the turning of history's wheels.

And yet something in that forgotten story clung to me. Back in England I had stumbled across her name in a fragment of research, the way you sometimes find a shard of pottery in a ploughed field. A broken piece, sharp and beautiful. They said she was the first woman ever hanged in New Mexico. The claim perhaps wasn't quite true, but her story is no less haunting.

They say she was young, beautiful. She loved a soldier named Miguel Martin - a man who, it turned out, already had a wife and five children. When he ended the affair, she drew a small knife and stabbed him. A crime of passion, betrayal, youth. At her trial, the defence pleaded for mercy, but the judge had no interest in mercy. She was tried for first degree murder, cold, premeditated murder.

That much I learned in England. But it was incomplete, uncertain, arcane, full of unanswered questions and that took hold of me. I could hear it like an old ballad, one of those slow, tragic songs that weave history and myth until you can't tell where one ends and the other begins. And so, when the road brought me to New Mexico, I followed her ghost to Las Vegas.

Las Vegas, New Mexico, is not the Vegas of neon lights and slot machines. It's another kind of show entirely. Once it was the terminus of the Santa Fe Trail, where wagon trains limped in from Missouri after months on the plains. Later it became a cattle town, its streets roaring with cowboys, gamblers, and outlaws. Wyatt Earp, Doc Holliday, Big Nose Kate, Billy the Kid - all of them passed through at one time or another.

But when I arrived, the wild days seemed long over, leaving only the shadows behind. The old buildings stood weathered but intact, their names still carved above doorways: E. Romero

Fire and Hose Company and Stern & Nahm Dry Goods. The Plaza Hotel still stands grand and sentinel. Doc Holliday had once shot a man in the saloon there, but all seemed peaceful and quiet when I went in, almost genteel.

I ate lunch in the hotel dining room. The manager told me about the old days as if they had just that moment passed by - how the trigger-happy dentist had his surgery just around the back and they had only recently got rid of the hole he had shot in the saloon. Back then Las Vegas and New Mexico as a whole was a witches' cauldron of mischief. What law there was could be bought. It was a time when a cartel of cattle barons would own everything in town including the sheriff. The federal government had little influence back then. In some parts of the territory (New Mexico wasn't a state back then) they sent in troops of Buffalo Soldiers - Afro -American soldiers - to try and keep a lid on things. The law was fluid, improvised and no-one knew from one day to the next who was really in charge.

I had hoped to learn more about Paula from the local museum, but when I got there the manager waved me away, claiming to be closed for cleaning. Disappointed, I wandered the streets looking for inspiration. Where would the memory of Paula hide? Not for the first time in my life I realised that the vagueness of my plan - in this case to find the ghost of someone who died over a 150 years ago - was a precursor to feeling lost and confused. And then, again not for the first time in my life, a door opened.

And I walked through it.

Wandering down the street, I came upon the Santa Fe Trail Association storefront, a modest place with photos and maps on the walls. It seemed to be the offices of some sort of local history group. At the back were two old men sitting on plastic chair talking.

And so, I met Leroy and Joe. Leroy Ledoux was small and dapper, with the manner of a man who still liked to look sharp. Joe Lopez was a big man wearing dungarees, impossibly old, his face a map of creases, tufts of white hair curling from ears and nose, his eyes red-rimmed and watery. He looked as though he had been sitting in that chair for a century, long enough to have seen everything come and go.

I stepped inside and introduced myself. “I’m over from England. I’m looking to find out more about someone called Paula Angel or Paula Angelo - do you know anything?”

Leroy raised an eyebrow, smiled. “Sure,” he said. “A bit. Come in and join us.” He stood up, walked to the door, and flipped the sign to Closed.

Rejoining us, we introduced ourselves. I introduced myself; Leroy introduced them both. “So,” he said, “how can we help?”

I told him about the story I heard and said I was trying to find out more about what had happened, to help me write a song or a book.

"Well, I know a bit, as I said, but I suspect Joe knows more," he said.

He turned back to Joe, speaking in Spanish, soft and coaxing. I couldn't catch every word, but I recognised the cadence of *¿Conoces la historia de Paula Angel?* Do you know the story of Paula Angel?

Joe sat motionless at first, as if the name hadn't landed. His hands were folded in his lap, his gaze fixed somewhere in the middle distance.

Leroy let him be. He started telling me about how his own family had started off as French-Canadian trappers working their way down west coast until presumably, they ran out of beavers and stopped.

And then Joe started speaking. His head lifted a fraction, and when he spoke it was in English, each word drawn out, heavy with age.

"She came from Loma Parda," he said. "It means Grey Hill. Wild place. Casino, bars. Soldiers used to fight with the ranchers. The men didn't like how the soldiers treated the women."

The words came haltingly, but with the peculiar authority of someone who seemed to be remembering rather than recounting. He hadn't been alive when Paula walked the earth, but the weight of his years made it feel possible. It was as if memory itself had seeped into him, and he was only now letting it rise to the surface.

Leroy nodded. "Loma Parda. They all went there. The soldiers. Closest place they could find a woman."

Between us we reconstructed her short tragic tale. The history is hazy, different characters appearing in different narratives. It's not even clear today how old Paula was when she died. Nineteen, perhaps. Maybe twenty-six, or twenty-seven. The reports differ. It isn't even clear what her true name was: Paula Angel in most accounts, but sometimes Pablita Martin. And yet, despite all the confusion, one thing is beyond doubt: on April 26, 1861, she became the first and last woman ever legally executed in New Mexico Territory.

She had stabbed her lover, Juan Miguel Martin, an officer at the nearby Fort Union, when he tried to end their affair. He was a married man, father of five, from a prominent family. She too came possibly from a family of standing. A *crime passionel*, the French would have called it: the kind of act that in almost any other jurisdiction at the time would not have led to the noose. Across America in the nineteenth century, juries shrank from executing women. Public opinion usually revolted at the thought. Most judges, most juries, found a way to show mercy.

But Paula had no such champion. The newspapers, preoccupied with the looming Civil War, barely reported her case.

The presiding judge was Kirby Benedict, a man known as much for whiskey as wisdom. He had been appointed by Abraham Lincoln himself. When officials later tried to have him removed, Lincoln replied: "Well, gentlemen, I know Benedict. We have been friends for over thirty years. He may imbibe to excess, but Benedict drunk knows more law than all the others on the bench in New Mexico sober. I shall not disturb him."

Benedict instructed the jury to consider only first-degree murder. No manslaughter, no crime of passion, no lesser charge. Only guilt or innocence, life or death. The jury found her guilty, and the death sentence was a given, Benedict refused to grant a stay of execution pending appeal. (Some have said, she *was* given leave to appeal but the execution day remained as it was, before the appeal might be heard.)

Her lawyer, Spruce McCoy Baird, was a Confederate sympathiser more interested in recruiting soldiers for looming civil war than in saving his client's life. Paula Angel was doomed.

The 'why' of all this has disappeared into history. Why murder in the first degree? Why no appeal? Why did the Sheriff - who was also the gaoler - taunt her every day up to her execution day, saying, “I am going to hang you till you’re dead, dead, dead”?

Her execution was improvised, like everything else on the frontier. No gallows had been built, so the sheriff chose a cottonwood tree just outside Las Vegas. Paula was tied to a wagon, made to ride to her death on top of her own coffin. Ranchers, townsfolk, and soldiers gathered to watch.

For weeks, the sheriff had taunted her: “I’m going to hang you till you’re dead, dead, dead.” On the day itself, he made a fatal blunder. He forgot to tie her hands.

The rope was looped over the branch, the wagon moved, and Paula, in a last desperate effort to live, forced her fingers between the noose and her throat. She clutched and struggled, her body writhing at the end of the rope. The crowd roared. Some jeered. Others cried out in protest, appalled at the spectacle. The sheriff grabbed at her, tried to pull her down, to hasten her end. The crowd turned ugly and amid chaos and catcalls, she was cut down.

And then came the extraordinary moment - the crowd started to argue about the outcome.

Was she already hanged? Had justice been served? Some in the crowd argued that she had paid the price. She had been hanged, had she not? The sentence had been carried out. Others demanded that the job be done “properly.” That she must die, not merely struggle. The sheriff hesitated, the crowd divided, the meaning of law itself dangling in the air like the rope above them.

It was a moment of pure frontier justice - where law was whatever the crowd decided, where justice was not written but improvised. The mob ruled in a place where reckoning was demanded, even if the rules had to be invented on the spot.

At last, the sheriff prevailed. Paula's hands and feet were bound. The rope was reset. The wagon pulled again. And this time there was no reprieve. Paula Angel died beneath the cottonwood tree, her story ending in confusion, cruelty, and silence.

That's how frontier justice worked - hurried, theatrical, tinged with whiskey. This wasn't about truth, or even about law. It was about performance. It was about control.

Then the conversation shifted. Leroy and Joe asked where I was from. Their knowledge of the British Isles was like for so many Americans hazy. I drew them a map of showing England, Scotland, Ireland, Wales. They were fascinated by the origins of the surnames in New Mexico. The truth is that the accents on the street back then would have reflected the diversity of the immigrants that were building the territory: Irish, Scots, Spanish, English, Afro-American, even German and Chinese. The American accent was still like the law round here: under construction.

They peppered me with questions: Jones, O'Neill? Higgins? Conway? Davis? Most of them I could hazard a guess at. Then "Where would Bonney come from?"

I didn't have a clue. But then I added, "Billy the Kid was a Bonney. William Bonney."

Joe said something.

"He's the Kid's third cousin," Leroy declared, almost with pride. "His grandfather knew him well."

I didn't have the heart to tell him that according to some, William Bonney was an alias, that the Kid had been born Henry McCarty. But then again, his mother had probably been born Catherine Bonney, so who knows? Perhaps it was not such an alias after all.

Joe leaned forward, his voice soft, almost conspiratorial. "He was a handsome man. Spanish ladies loved him." He showed me a piece of paper that contained his family tree and his relationship to Bonney family through his mother's side.

I felt I could almost touch the intangible - that he might be standing there, or sitting across the room in the bar of the Plaza hotel. It was like realising that Robin Hood was standing at the bar with you in the Coaches and Horses, or King Arthur was in the queue at the chip shop. Or Princess Lea from Star Wars was in the laundromat.

America does that to you. The myth of it is so 'real' after a lifetime of film, TV and gaming that it is shock to find it is really real.

By now I could tell Joe was getting tired so I bade the two of them cheerio, leaving them to their old maps, and documents and family trees. I was going to head out to Loma Parda and look some more for the ghost of Paula Angel and with a bit of luck I would get there before sundown.

Later on in a road trip, I drove down to Fort Sumner to see Billy's grave. It's surrounded by iron bars now - to keep people from stealing the headstone. Someone had left red roses there. Someone still loves the old outlaw. Although presumably not the relatives of the nearby grave whose grave hold the remains, it states, of one who was shot by William Bonney.

Billy the Kid has spent more than a century in the crosshairs of myth. To some, he's the pistol-wielding psychopath of dime novels; to others, the reckless saint of the dispossessed - the boy outlaw with a grin and a gun, riding forever through the dusty dreams of America. But strip away the legend and you don't find a monster or a hero - just a kid caught in the undertow of a broken world. Born Henry McCarty, raised in poverty, orphaned before he was grown, abandoned by his stepfather, he drifted from boarding house to boarding house along the hard edge of the frontier - a land where justice was bought by the rich and survival was the only law that mattered. His first crime was to steal food.

When the Lincoln County War broke out, he didn't join for glory. He took sides because loyalty still meant something. The 'Regulators' he rode with weren't the pure villains the newspapers claimed - they were standing up to a corrupt monopoly that owned the land, the cattle, even the sheriffs. Billy was nineteen: bright, restless, fast on the draw, and trapped in the chaos of the times, he found he had no way out.

He killed, yes, and we shouldn't flinch from that. But look closer, and you see a young man writing to the Governor, asking for a pardon, trying to make peace, trying to step out of the story already written for him. When the law betrayed him, he ran - not because he loved the chase, but because he'd lost faith in the rules of the game.

That's what lingers. The humanity. The sense of someone trapped in the whirligig.

The sad, bizarre but compelling stories of Paula Angel and Billy the Kid show some of the strands of the America we know emerging from the crucible of its unique story. The Old West was a place where there was no safety and no one to call on for protection except the others in your community. A place where the level of support might be arbitrary and based on personal like and dislike, in group and out rather than any sense of a rule. There was justice without law, and punishment without regard, and guilt without reason.

It was less of a justice system and more of a moral theatre, based on the Puritan ideas of evil needing a reckoning and redemption demanding blood and sacrifice. Public vengeance was cathartic, satiating the craving for purification rather than the cool logic of rehabilitation. It was a visceral hunger for action and retribution.

And did America learn from this, and is this why the gun remains such a totemic symbol? In a legal vacuum the individual becomes the final arbiter of right and wrong. Does this line of reasoning run from the Salem Witch Trials to the fascination for vigilante superheroes?

At the killing of one so young
While another's baking bread.

That's how it must have felt. A girl hanged in the morning, and by the afternoon life resumed. Horses fed, bread baked, drinks poured. Justice improvised, life carried on.

And then she was forgotten. The Civil War broke out within weeks. Newspapers barely glanced her way. Decades passed before her name surfaced again, when local historians pieced fragments together. For nearly a century there was doubt she had even been executed at all - until the discovery of the sheriff's handwritten confirmation on the back of the warrant.

Meanwhile, Billy the Kid's grave at Fort Sumner became a shrine. Roses still appear there. His myth flourished because it suited the legend: the young outlaw, handsome, dangerous, doomed. Paula Angel left no roses, no shrine. Her death was too messy, too female, too unromantic for the myth.

And yet her story may tell us more about America than Billy's ever did. Because in that bungled hanging - cut down, debated, strung up again - you can see the genesis of the American myth: law and theatre, reckoning and spectacle, injustice wrapped in the guise of order.

The frontier was a place where lawmen were often half-outlaw, and outlaws dreamed of justice. Wyatt Earp, lionised as the upright marshal of Tombstone, was just as often an opportunist. Wild Bill Hickok was a lawman, a gambler, a gunfighter, and a showman. Pat Garrett, who killed Billy the Kid, was praised as a defender of law and condemned as an executioner.

Paula doesn't fit among them. She wasn't glamorous. She wasn't mythic. She was young, betrayed, and silenced. But precisely because she doesn't fit, she forces us to look harder. She forces us to ask what 'justice' meant in a world still inventing the word.

Reckoning sits deep in the American soul. It is more than punishment - it is the moment a story is judged, the account settled. But Paula had no reckoning, only a sentence. And yet, in telling her story now, perhaps we grant her one at last.

Such deeds and songs are rambling on
In the American wilderness...

Billy has roses. Paula has silence. And in that silence, the myth of America was forged. Out of bungled justice, improvised law, and unfinished stories, a legend was born - a legend that still rides today.

The ghosts keep coming. Through desert and canyon, through courthouse and saloon. Not demanding agreement, only attention. And they ask us the same question they asked that crowd under the cottonwood tree:

When the reckoning comes... who will you be?

Intermission: American Wilderness

He was a Yankee soldier brave, Miguel Martin was his name.
A soldier in a uniform with the ladies he found fame.
They say she was an angel fair but one who'd fell so low.
Each night as the sun went down, to the old creek they would go.

She loved him true, she loved him well,
through the summer's night.
'Til they heard the bugle calling as the day began to light.
One day she said "Will you fly with me to a land so far away?"
He kissed her on her lovely hair, and told her he would stay.

Such deeds and songs are rambling on
In the American wilderness

"You know it's true, I swear it's true, with you I'd love to roam.
But did I forget to mention my five kids left at home?"
Her eyes grew wide, her blood did race,
drew a dagger from her dress.
"It seems that I must end the days of the one I loved the best."

And the bugle called and his brother came,
as she kissed his life away.
They dragged her to the courthouse to await her judgement day.

Such deeds and songs are rambling on
In the American wilderness

Benedict was a travelling judge with whisky on his breath.
He said "Let's get this over with, before I bore myself to death."
He said "Most like you can appeal,
but I won't stay the hanging day.
Let's hear the next one on my list, I'd best be on my way."

Such deeds and songs are rambling on
In the American wilderness

The gaoler had a vicious mind. Each morn, she'd hear him say:
"Gonna hang you 'til you're dead, dead, dead!
'Til then it's here, you'll stay."
What it was that grew such hate, guess we'll never know.
What is true was on that day he drove that cart real slow.

Such deeds and songs are rambling on
In the American wilderness

On the Main Street down in Vegas, there gathered such a crowd
To see an angel on a coffin whose lovely head was bowed.
But not all were there to shout or stare,
for the beat of life goes on,
And tragedy is but a moment's breath ,the cartwheel's carillon.

Such deeds and songs are rambling on
In the American wilderness

So Caleb brushed down broken horses with sorrow on his mind
He'd seen too many bad times to be the watching kind
And a drifter saw the empty gaol then stole away to sleep,
And Lilith took another drink, her memories to keep.

> *Such deeds and songs are rambling on*
> *In the American wilderness*

Silas stayed to knead the dough but wondered in his head,
At the killing of one so young while another's baking bread.

> *Such deeds and songs are rambling on*
> *In the American wilderness*

Over in that dirt dust square, the gaoler he did smirk.
Took a bow to those gathered there, and went about his work

Getting to the hanging tree, he forgot to tie her well.
So when the cart he drove away, and to the earth she fell,
Her hands were free to grasp the noose
that tightened round her throat
The gaoler grasped her round the waist, her ending to promote.

> *Such deeds and songs are rambling on*
> *In the American wilderness*

The crowd grew chilled and said out loud:
"For God's sake, let her be!
This ain't how it's done round here. She's hanged so set her free."
And so they cut her down right there,
laid her gasping on the ground.
Some of them said the day was done,
but one man turned them round.

Such deeds and songs are rambling on
In the American wilderness

And with his tongue, he stilled the crowd,
and this is what he said:
"It wasn't just a hanging crime, but a hanging till she's dead."
And so It was that the angel died. The town it moved along.
The gaoler took the story home, most felt he'd done her wrong.

Such deeds and songs are rambling on
In the American wilderness

Listen online: arcr.uk/gtlfamusic

Chapter 9: Sodom on the Mora

Leroy and Joe had pointed me here. Sitting in that dusty little Santa Fe Trail Association office in Las Vegas, they told me Paula Angel had come from Loma Parda. Grey Hill. A wild place. Soldiers from Fort Union would ride down to it when they wanted drink or women. Miguel Martin, the man Paula loved and killed, had been stationed at the fort. The more I listened, the clearer it became: if I wanted to understand Paula's story, I needed to see this place for myself.

Ghost towns in New Mexico are not rare. The state is littered with over 400 of them - silent, sun-bleached testaments to ambition, grit, and collapse. Some, like Madrid or Chloride, are part-museum, part-art-project. Others have been swallowed entirely by the desert. They are places of rust and ruin where the wind carries whispers and doors bang in houses that no longer have roofs. Each one a story half-finished, a dream eroded by time, or a town broken by the turning of economic wheels elsewhere, of half-collapsed mining camps, abandoned trading posts, railroad stops that never made it, and blow-off towns like this one that outlived their soldiers.

Loma Parda once had a reputation so sordid it earned the nickname *Sodom on the Mora*. It was supposedly the wildest, baddest outpost on the frontier - a magnet for vice, whiskey, gambling, and women, not to mention violence.

I left Las Vegas heading northeast on Interstate 25, then turned off toward the Mora River valley. Within a short while, the metalled roads gave way to dirt, and I bounced along through the late-afternoon light across a wide plain where a few cattle and horses grazed. The road jostled my van and blurred the line between where I was and when I was. Turning off onto another even more rough-hewn track I headed down a steepening valley, my route lined on both sides by tree and bush, of juniper and pine. The road more or less petered out just before a narrow bridge. Pulling over I got out and walked across it. The bridge ran over a sparkling creek, and in the dappling light, where the evening sun shone through the trees, I saw them: a herd of buffalo, a few of the once many but still magnificent, clustered at the water's edge. They lifted their heads as I passed, massive, indifferent, ancient. One of them turned to look at me with sorrowful eyes.

Moving on, I found that the broken bones of the old town remained. Along with what I assumed was the old Main Street lay the remnants of houses, saloons and stores, most, at best with a couple of walls still standing. Their timbers fell at angles propping up the blockwork and in turn being propped up by them, like a couple of old drunks hanging onto each other to stay upright. Sometimes the windows still had wooden surrounds, but the glass was long gone, ground into the dirt beneath my feet.

Walking up the street I peered into houses trying to sense, feel, absorb the past. I stopped in one doorway, running my hand across the wall. The surface flaked away at the lightest touch, leaving a trace of earth on my fingers. Inside, a beam of light cut through a gap in the roof, making the dust hang like smoke. I tried to imagine the room lit by lamplight and filled with voices, laughter, music, and then a gunshot or two. Ghosts don't always need to show themselves; they just mutter in the shadows of sundown.

So, this was the place where Paula Angel once smiled flirtatiously or shyly, we will never know, at a handsome officer in the US Army. Where he, confident in his uniform and his years, smiled back. It's easy to imagine them in that dry country twilight, meeting by the river as bugles called in the distance. A brief love, a betrayal, a crime born of heartbreak. A story that might have remained private had not the town, the judge, the soldiers, and the frontier itself needed it to become spectacle.

As I stood in contemplation it struck me that here was another America. Not the one of grand thesis and exposition but a kaleidoscope America, where brief stories rise like the grit in the breeze of time, sparkle for a while in the sunlight, then drift away back into the void. No great causal flow explaining everything, just fragile moments, patterns of love and loss, courage and cruelty. The cracked walls and wind-scoured timbers seemed to breathe the elusive memory of all that had passed: laughter, rage, the creak of saddle leather, the faint music from some long-vanished saloon. All that remains now are the shades of stories without endings dissolving into forgetfulness and silence.

And then I heard it. The unmistakable sound of a child laughing, clear as a bell in the still air. Ghosts? The real thing?

Then came the apparition. A quad bike was making its way toward me, a young boy at the controls and a beautiful, slim woman riding behind him. They pulled up beside me, a little wary, a little amused.

"If I find you here, you must be lost," she said with a smile.

I told her a little about what I was trying to do, a writer trying to understand what had happened in this once-notorious place. She looked me over again, then said, "Well, there's plenty of stories round here. But I'm just visiting. My fiancé's father lives here. He's eighty-seven. His family's been here forever. Come and meet him."

"Are you sure it's okay?" I asked.

"Sure. He's on his own most of the time. He loves visitors. Come on."

We turned back toward the homestead I'd passed earlier, a ramshackle collection of sheds and outbuildings patched together over generations, all wearing a large bolt or padlock. We walked up to find him - an elderly man in the doorway of a low, rough-hewn house, the yard scattered with tools, timber, and old machinery, the porch shaded by a patchwork of tin and timber. He was short, stocky, weathered - like a fencepost that had stood too many seasons. He wore jeans, a T-shirt, a sleeveless black gilet, and a working man's cap.

The dark-eyed girl introduced me and told him I was looking to find out more about Loma Parda.

He looked me over with interest seasoned with a little suspicion. He sized me up and shook my hand like it mattered.

"I'm a bit busy at the moment, got my family here, but if you come back here tomorrow, I might have something."

So, the next morning I returned and met properly: Ben C de Baca.

"De Baca means cow's head," he told me, laughing as we sat on old chairs in a little lean-to full of old books, stacks of magazines and VHS cassettes. "My people came with the first

Spanish settlers. We've been here since before the others came."

Turns out he really knew the place; his family had been here for generations. He waved toward the ruins.

"My family owned that saloon, and that one over there was the gambling house. The McMartins had the hotel and the corral. We had a horse-drawn taxi service back then - ran the soldiers from the Fort down here to the fun."

He was a storyteller, alright. But there was nothing rehearsed about him. He didn't embellish. He remembered.

"That bar was open 24 hours a day. The taxi service too. You could walk in anytime and find someone passed out, someone shouting, and someone falling in love or starting a fight."

He showed me old clippings from newspapers and newsletters. Some tried to downplay the town's reputation. Others leaned into it.

The favourite drink was a local rotgut called "Loma Lightning." Sharp, smoky, and dangerous. And the game of choice? Three-card monte. Fast hands, fast money, and faster regrets. Ben smiled as he told me, "My great-uncle used to light his cigarettes with dollar bills. Real show-off. People thought he was crazy. He probably was."

I asked him about Paula Angel. He looked a bit evasive. "I don't remember much," he said.

"Did she come from here?"

Again, a pause.

"Perhaps... yes."

Later, I found a copy of *Haunted Highways*, by Ralph Looney, who visited Loma Parda in 1968. His account resonated with Ben's stories.

Fort Union itself was enormous, the largest military post in the Southwest - barracks, warehouses, a hospital, workshops, even a bakery turning out thousands of loaves. At its peak, more than three thousand soldiers were stationed there. But discipline could not compete with temptation. Men slipped away under cover of night, drawn by music and laughter drifting up the valley. Some deserted entirely, preferring Loma Parda's chaos to the fort's order.

Life at Fort Union had been as regimented as Loma Parda was chaotic. Soldiers rose at dawn to bugle calls, lined up for drill, ate hard biscuits and salt pork from government stores. They patched uniforms, repaired wagons, and hauled water in endless routines. There were rules for everything - when to march, when to eat, when to sleep. Pay came late, food was dull, and punishments were harsh.

Loma Parda was the inversion of that world. No bugles, no sergeants, no marching columns - just the lure of whiskey, women, and cards. In place of ration lines, there were dice tables; in place of roll call, music spilling from saloon doors. It's no wonder men slipped away, even knowing desertion could bring the lash or the firing squad. Between the two worlds - order and chaos - most men chose chaos at least once.

Little Sodom proved a crown of thorns for the post commanders at the Fort. Among other things, the town proved to be a convenient cache for loot stolen from the post. Gen. James H. Carlton at one point sought to have his quartermaster lease the town, after which he planned on its 'legal' destruction.

Things got so wild in 1866 that the new commanding officer, Major John Thomson, declared Loma Parda off-limits. A brawl on May 10 had left two soldiers badly wounded. Thomson's report claimed the locals had attacked them "without any provocation," and he called on the mayor to arrest the culprits.

The mayor replied by demanding that Thomson hand over several soldiers accused of breaching the peace. Sensing a trap but unwilling to provoke open conflict, Thomson sent the request on to Santa Fe, wryly noting that if granted, "this post will largely be represented at that place, and the soldiers will be detained so long as a dollar, or dollar's worth of property, can be gleaned from them."

The mayor, meanwhile, acted first - arresting and disarming the very detachment Thomson had sent to restore order. He held them for a spell, then released them on his own terms, telling Lieutenant Thomas Clancy exactly what he thought of military authority:

“I do not care a damn for you, the commanding officer, or any other military authority, and I will turn them loose when I get through with them, and after that they can go where they damn please.”

It’s hard to imagine a clearer statement of how the citizens of Loma Parda felt about the US Army.

In general, you might say Loma Parda represented the unruly independence of much the American character. With less restraint you might say it was a good example of America unhinged!

One account of the times really caught my eye. The *Las Vegas Optic* carried a story about a killer named James Lafer. Riding into Loma Parda he picked up a young Mexican woman in the street, swung her up across his saddle, and rode straight into the saloon. Ordering drinks for everyone, he demanded the bartender serve his horse first. When the poor beast wouldn’t drink, Lafer calmly drew his gun and shot it through the head. Before the horse hit the floorboards, he lifted the woman down from the saddle and walked out into the sun, leaving the dead animal in a pool of dust and silence.

In another incident a post at Fort Union read:

"A report has just come to us that a murder was committed on Sunday last, 9 October, 1871... A man lies dead in the bushes close by, about one mile from the village near the partita. Horses were saddled and several men dispatched... The dead man was found without clothing, which seems to have been the motive, what a crime! To kill a man for the clothes on his back. The dead man was named Bergman. He belonged to the Eighth Cavalry stationed at the Fort. His head was beaten to jelly by stones. His clothes were sorely wanted."

But it wasn't just soldiers and locals who stirred things up in Little Sodom on the Mora, for bands of Comancheros roamed around the hills and plains that surrounded it. These were Hispanic and mixed heritage settlers who originally got their name by trading with the Comanche Indians. They lived wild lives, with one foot on either side of the law and if a few 'lost' cattle ended up their possession, well that was just good fortune. Texas cowhands working to bring steers to market did not agree. It was rumoured that Comanchero gangs kept much of their gains in Loma Parda. On one occasion a bunch of Texans decided to ride into town and reclaim their lost animals.

The Texans quickly rounded up seven steers. They were about to leave when some of the Loma Pardans levelled their guns and took the cattle back. But the Texans weren't about to let the Loma 'Mexes' get the better of them.

About twenty of them returned the next day. Again, the locals barred their way with rifles. Again, the Texans backed off. Soon the Texans came once more to Loma Parda - this time sixty strong. Swarming across the Mora River and up Little Sodom's main street, they rode straight to the home of Julian Baca and demanded to see his corral.

Inside, they spotted two horses they claimed were stolen and ordered Baca to hand them over. He refused, saying he had bills of sale. The cowboys beat him black and blue.

The Loma Parda version says that Baca's wife ran screaming into the street. Help came quickly in the form of Toribio Garcia, who lived across the way. He grabbed a six-shooter and ran to the Baca house. But when the Texans turned their guns on him, he dropped his pistol and tried to flee. A cowboy's bullet caught him in the back, and he fell dead in the dust.

Just another day in town. It was easy see with all this tension and conflict how Paula's story might have been shaped. Perhaps the anger of her lover's comrades had led to the strange process of her trial and execution. Perhaps she was like Capulets and the Montagues, just associated with the wrong family, a victim of revenge in some sort of vendetta or feud.

Ben told me that eventually Fort Union shut down. No more soldiers, no more money. Little Sodom became once again the place on the Grey Hill.

Life changed then, and families tried to replace the lost garrison money with trees and patience, an afterlife of apples and apricots where saloons had once roared.

“We had fruit orchards once, you know. This valley was full of them. The gardens were beautiful.”

“What happened?” I asked.

“They took it. Sanchez. Dr. Brown. They tricked the people into signing away the land. Said they were helping. Bastards.”

He said it like it still hurt. And it did. Then came the mysterious fire. Then the road to town was blocked. The buildings were torched. Even the gravestones thrown into the river. Ben had been working in Denver at the time. He returned to find ruin. But he stayed. Rebuilt what he could. Fought the State authorities and everyone else. Kept the fight going against “them.”

And that’s how he said it. Always “they.” “Them.” A shadowy group - sometimes bureaucrats, sometimes corporations, sometimes government men, cartels. Like the cattle barons who once ran Lincoln County and much of the west with magnificent corruption.

And Ben has kind of won. The lone gunman staring down band of thugs who have come to take away his home. He got permission stay. Even begrudgingly the road was opened up a bit so he could get in and out. Now his family come and stay with caravans and building cabins of their own reclaiming a little of what went before.

And, judging by the boxes of letters and documents in his lean-to Ben fights on.

I drove away thinking about how these ghost towns haunt us because they once pulsed with life. They speak to the fragility of things we think are solid. They remind us that people out here have always been dancing on a cliff edge - chasing dreams, breaking rules, building worlds that could never last. Another turn of the kaleidoscope.

Dawson, once the largest mining town in New Mexico, was erased almost overnight after the mine disasters of 1913 and 1923 - hundreds killed, families scattered, a town that simply vanished from the map. Out along Route 66, whole rows of motels and gas stations were abandoned when the interstate bypassed them. Neon signs still stand in the desert, glowing only when lightning flashes. In the Dust Bowl years, whole farmsteads in eastern New Mexico were left to the dust, houses buried by drifts of soil, furniture still inside.

The West has always been a boom-and-bust machine. Gold, silver, copper, cattle, railroads -each promised permanence, each collapsed when the seams ran dry or the tracks moved on. Ghost towns are the ledger left behind: each ruin a line written in the book of ambition.

In this vast landscape it seems our lives are just tumbleweed blown along by a capricious wind. Our stories, like Paula's, brief.

Intermission: Interstate 25

I was somewhere in a sea of gold in the pirate town of Vegas
Which had summoned all the good folks there
to follow like the Magus
I was weary of my new friend's whine, the days were going slow
So I thought that I might cut and run to the state of New Mexico

The shadow of a crow, the tumbleweed's alive.
Hawk is sweeping low on the Interstate 25.

Where the moon it rises like the wolf, to howl on the desert's edge.
The lion she calls on all below, to take the ancient pledge.
The whiptail thinks and waits, under the shade of a fiery stone.
The roadrunner stops to catch its breath
on the trail of Al Capone.

The shadow of a crow, the tumbleweed's alive.
Hawk is sweeping low on the Interstate 25.

To a ghost town down the beaten track
where a brown-eyed girl is sayin':
"If I find you here, you must be lost,
but I don't mind you stayin'."
The hotel's just an empty shell,
the casino's wheel stopped spinning.
The sweet ladies all went home,
the gambler took his winnings.

The shadow of a crow, the tumbleweed's alive.
Hawk is sweeping low on the Interstate 25.

"The doctor was a skunk so rare,
he sold our lives forever.
They even burned the old church down,
threw the tombstones in the river!"
As I drove away from that lonely place,
"brown eyes" winked and waved
I wondered how and in what ways
us sinners might be saved?

The shadow of a crow, the tumbleweed's alive.
Hawk is sweeping low on the Interstate 25.

Listen online: arcr.uk/gtlfamusic

Chapter 10: Laissez Les Bons Temps Rouler

I am prone to a little exaggeration perhaps, but I do feel every time I pack up to leave New Orleans, I am like an alien who has been allowed to return to the mothership for a few days. I am always going to be comfortable in a world that is inconsistent, improvised and shapeshifting. At its best, the Big Easy distils everything America could be.

Hell, once it was a Monday night and as I walked back from a Creole Italian restaurant there was a band playing in the middle of the street. A man in a car, windows open, stared at the stars and waited for them to finish before driving on. No honking the horn, no shouting abuse from a wound-down window, no reaching for a gun.

Things aren't compartmentalised there; everything co-habits simultaneously. A few inches above a rising sea level it exists while it can exist, focusing on the hour ahead, embracing diversity and having a hell of a time. It is stoicism with a smile and glass of the aptly named Hurricane (a blend of light and dark rum, passion fruit syrup and lime).

The love affair started on day one of my first visit. Of course, I woke ridiculously early after the flight from England. It must have been 3:30am. I half-dozed for a while but gave up at about 5:45am, had a bath, unpacked a few things, and then headed off to explore. I couldn't help thinking that the last place I had been that looked like this, with its sunburnt olives, ochres, russet and saffron, was Cartagena in Colombia (without the background threat you feel there). It was great to walk around the gridiron streets which, apart from the geometry, felt provocatively un-American.

I was amused to find a bar, the Golden Lantern, open and offering 'The world's best Bloody Mary' and a blackboard suggesting you skip breakfast. It was open, and I peered through the door; a number of cheerful-looking men sitting around looked up and smiled waving me in, seemingly early birds rather than leftovers from the night before. I looked the place up on the internet later when I got back - apparently it was a 24/7 gay bar.

So it began. I was fortunate in New Orleans on that visit to have as my sometime guide Dr. Michael J. Apter. Mike was one of those rare figures who seemed to live three or four lives at once: an eminent psychologist, fluent in French, an aficionado of jazz, a collector of antique Americana, and, in one of his more unexpected chapters, a bar owner in Spain. He had once married in Versailles Palace, counted John Cleese among his schoolboy friends, and remained gloriously hopeless at golf.

He could list Yale, Chicago, and Georgetown among his visiting professorships, yet in New Orleans, where he then lived with his wife Mitzi, he was more interested in wandering into bookshops in search of obscure French philosophy, or baiting a hoity-toity antiques dealer with the aplomb of a man who enjoyed puncturing pomposity. As idiosyncratic a companion as you could hope for, he drifted through the city with a mix of professorial gravity and mischievous delight - the perfect foil for a visitor like me.

On that first trip I sat in tree-shaded squares at lunchtime and drank beer, talked of philosophy and psychology, and listened to jazz. I rode on a steamboat, a paddle steamboat that went up the muddy Mississippi. Okay, it was a replica built in 1975, but the steam engines were real and very old. I ate alligator sausage and smelt the sweet scent of the world's second-biggest sugar refinery - a blackened, ruined, decaying business. The sight of it meant I couldn't help thinking of the darker past of New Orleans, the plantations, the sugarcane, the slavery and the servitude that had brought so many people there.

I went to a voodoo museum, two rooms filled with the mundane and the bizarre, and a darkened corridor of fading photographs and newsprint, which I read by the light of my smartphone.

Mike was an expert collector of art and antiques. He was very keen we spend a while in the expensive antique shops and galleries in which I could be no more than an uninterested observer. We went to one full of grand, heavy, bombastic European furniture from a couple of centuries ago. I was sure the pile in the carpet was so deep it tickled my knees, though it may have been that I had fallen into ancestral servile posture. Mike sparred awhile with a slim lady in a tailored black dress about Louis XV furniture. He used bumbling half-interest and she insistent politeness as swords of combat. She tried to steer him towards what she thought he should see, and he resisted, like an old bear refusing to do tricks.

Further up the street he headed into a well-heeled art gallery. Toulouse-Lautrec posters were in the window, sculptures of petite-bosomed young women floated in giant leaves, Picasso drawings, and Chagall sketches. Again, the sizing up of opportunity, capacity and interest.

We went book shopping and we found a bookshop, Arcadia, which felt like something out of a novel itself. Books piled from floor to ceiling, many face down in pillars and columns, row upon row, wall upon wall like a levee of books.

"I bet you know where everything is," I said to the owner.

"I certainly do," came the urbane reply.

I picked up a print of New Orleans I really liked. On the back it said it was by a French artist, Jeremie Garcin, who had come to New Orleans for a short visit and stayed three months, drawing people and places. It said a book of his drawings had been published.

"I don't suppose you have the book?" I asked.

"I certainly do," said the urbane owner, and went straight for it.

Mike asked if he had a book by the French philosopher Diderot, *Le Rêve d'Alembert*, a Socratic dialogue of the 18th century, which apparently included one of the protagonists providing a hand job to the other (one way of settling an argument, I suppose) written in French. The urbane reply was:

"I certainly do!"

And he did.

I drank beer and coffee and ate beignets and crawfish and shrimp and walked. Everywhere there was music: down Frenchmen's we listened in the Spotted Cat and the Bamboula. Through my open window earlier that day, as I started to write, I could hear someone playing sax, the honk-deep goose sound of a railway whistle, the occasional clank of a streetcar bell, and the steam-driven pipes of a calliope playing ragtime.

It is a swamp, a wilderness, a fair and a circus.

I would live there if I could, in the French Quarter somewhere around Chartres and Barracks Streets so I could enjoy the walk in. A first or second-floor apartment with old French doors opening onto a wrought-iron veranda, from which bougainvillea and geraniums cascaded in drunken delight. Passing the daylight hours writing books and living off coffee and beignets, after a few hundred words I would head down to the French Market - founded, I believed, by the Spanish.

The market is down by the river and the rail track, once a trading post with local native tribes. Colonnades held up a wooden roof against the sun and the rain, under which dark-eyed ladies, Creole kids and men and women with history in their faces sold food rich in wandering and ancestry: crawfish and alligator pies, po'boys laden with fried oyster, jambalaya, snowballs, gumbo, crepes, soft-shell crab supported by dirty rice and beans.

The food of America had always been one of its most eccentric calling cards. This was, after all, a nation that invented the popsicle, bubble-gum, Philadelphia Cream Cheese, chocolate brownies, Corn Flakes, Twinkies, TV dinners, the Big Mac and... wait for it... fudge. A roll call that might give you cause for concern if you took it as the national diet.

But New Orleans is something else entirely. Here, food feels like a kind of inventive witchcraft. It takes the dark, the mysterious, the ancient and arcane, and somehow serves it steaming and delicious on a plate. It was food with ancestry, food with mischief, food that laughed at neat categories and embraced the idea that everything belonged in the pot.

And again, always there is the music. It is metaphor and a cipher for what lies at the heart of the place.

On another visit trying a plate of Crayfish Louis and a beer in the French Market, I sat under some Cypress trees drinking and listening to Jimmy Bean Bolero play some earthy but fluent rhythm and blues. Something clicked and the whole illusion fell away and behind the curtain lay the whole spice box of music - African, Spanish, Creole, German, Catholic, Puritan, and on and on, It made me think just how much damn music had been invented there in that gumbo of nations and cultures.

New Orleans can, without blushing, claim to have invented a fair slice of modern music. Jazz was born here - not just one kind of jazz, but the whole sprawling family: from the ragged exuberance of trad to the brass swagger of New Orleans style, to the dizzy flights of bebop and the cool experiments that followed. Rhythm and blues, too, took shape in these streets, hammered out by the likes of Fats Domino and Professor Longhair, laying down the grooves that would soon become rock 'n' roll. Even gospel, in its modern, pulsing form, owed something to the city's spirituals and sanctified choirs. And later, of course, funk swaggered out of New Orleans with The Meters and their like, a rhythm so greasy it could slip through your fingers.

But the influence didn't stop at what was born there. The city acted as a kind of musical ferment, sending its yeast out into the wider world. The blues took on new colours after passing through New Orleans ears. Rock 'n' roll - though often claimed by Memphis - leaned heavily on the R&B coming out of the Crescent City. Soul, swing, honkytonk, even country found themselves sharpened or sweetened by the touch of that city.

So if America gave the world an explosion of styles in a single century - ragtime , rock 'n' roll, hip-hop, country, bluegrass, folk, punk, disco and more - then New Orleans could reasonably say: hell, we started the party, and we kept the band playing.

If diversity and variety are the ingredients of this magic then freedom, expressed as the thrill of unselfconscious exuberance is the incantation, the summoning that makes the sorcery work.

The French Market may now be a siren for the tourists but as I wandered through the place signs of this exuberance were everywhere. Here you could get your name written on a piece of rice, buy a piece of wood that let your plant pots defy gravity, a leather handbag in the shape of a turtle, take chess lessons in the sun with a grandmaster. A man could put down his hat upon the floor and unaccompanied start singing *I Got Sunshine on a Cloudy Day*, and people would put money in it.

Walking along a little further to the great square, to Bourbon Street, past the voodoo shops lining up with dark bars, fine art galleries and a shop that sold nothing but Tabasco sauce in a hundred varieties. Along streets where people played mysterious many-stringed instruments and back into Arcadia, where all the dusty books of the world were piled in vertical columns and an urbane bookseller still knew where every single one was.

In all my years of travels, I thought New Orleans stood out as one of those places where the diverse tapestry of humanity was lived out in its glorious potential. An old traveller was moved to write:

"As for the confusion of tongues in the market, it was simply delicious. French, Italian, Spanish, Portuguese, Dutch and 'Gumbo' contended with each other for supremacy. There were Gascon butchers, the Italian and Spanish fruit vendors and the German vegetable women. There were Moors, with their strings of beads and crosses, fresh from the Holy Land, Chinese and Hindu, Jew and Teuton, French and Creole, Malay, Irish and English, all uniting in a ceaseless babble of tongues that was simply bewildering."

That evening, I sat in a restaurant, the windows open to the streets outside. There was the sound of music, horns honking. An open-topped limo came into view surrounded by a group of dancing, laughing people throwing strings of black beads to passers-by. Death stood up in the back in a skeleton suit, tailcoat and tall hat on his head. He was laughing maniacally.

That was the thing about New Orleans - even Old Death and the dead were welcome and reliable guests, hanging out in the courtyards and side streets, appearing on parade and just generally moseying around.

This was the magic dream of America, a place where you could flourish, dance and sing, glorious in your difference and contradiction. It was where all the stories of the whole world wove themselves into a rug of hope.

Don't get me wrong, New Orleans is still haunted by a dark and troubled past. A place where removing statues and monuments that celebrated slavers and apologists was still bitterly regretted by many. This was not Chuck Berry's 'Promised Land' - he passed through there on his way to something better.

But at its best, New Orleans is perhaps proof of concept of the potential for a self-determining, self-reliant people prepared to listen, appreciate and indeed love one another. The jazz music created in that great city, which I listened to sitting in the balmy evening drinking a last-of-the-day beer, captured it: the contradiction of improvisation and structure brought together in a common purpose, a shared heartbeat and a vision.

This is *New* Orleans, a city forever reinventing itself in song, gumbo, and the stubborn belief that life could always start again, even in the shadow of death.

It struck me how often America had reached for that word, as if it were a magic charm. New Mexico. New Hampshire. New Jersey. New York. New Orleans. To stand up in the world, this country kept baptising itself afresh, declaring that whatever had gone before could be shaken off and replaced.

But 'new' was never clean. It was a palimpsest - one story painted over another, old marks bleeding through. What you saw in America was rarely brand new. It was reinvention: layers of memory and myth colliding with the present.

And nowhere did that seem truer than New Orleans: a city that wore its history like a carnival mask - sequins, feathers, trumpet blasts on the outside, but always with the eyes and bones of something older showing through.

Intermission:
Silver Moon, Silver Girl

I drank so deep from seven wells,
  said "Come on girl, let's give 'em hell!"
They're waiting for the final bell,
  sold their souls as far as I can tell.
Give me a taste of 'Something fine'.

The world out there is catching fire,
  That old damn mule has lost a tyre.
The angels and the saints conspire,
  to leave me just a gun for hire
So give me a taste of 'Something fine'.

  Silver moon, silver girl. Take me to Cimarron.
  Silver moon, silver girl. Route 66 or Santa Fe,
  Mountains high or broken way, live to love another day,
  Keep on, keeping on!

I couldn't if I wanted to, tear it up and start anew.
Take another point of view, steal my heart right back from you.
Give me a taste of 'Something fine'.

The bad girls and the vampire set,
the waterboys who ain't spoke yet,
The piano man who placed a bet,
who could not lose he's so in debt.
Give me a taste of "Something fine."

That mules tail, well, it played a drum.
I took a drink so I'm feeling numb.
Won't spare a dime for another bum,
I'm laying low and keeping dumb.
'Til you give me a taste of 'Something fine'.

On the lazy ridge at the edge night,
side by side in failing light.
Something crazy, something right.
"Shall I stop here? Well, I think I might."
Give me a taste of 'Something fine'.

That west coast song went round my head,
it found its way to my big wide bed.
When the heart is hollow… it's easily led.

Listen online: arcr.uk/gtlfamusic

Chapter 11: Western Requiem

After ten chapters of searching, wandering, and digging through the myth and muck of America, you might think the journey is done. And in a sense, it is. Chapter Ten felt like the end, the circle closing back on itself.

So why this chapter? Why keep going? Because every journey has an after-echo. A coda. A last riff, played out in the half-light when the crowd has thinned, the amps are cooling, and the ghosts are still dancing in the corner. That's what this is: my Western Requiem.

When I wrote the song of the same name, I wasn't aiming for a history lesson. It was more a scrapbook of images that had haunted me since boyhood afternoons watching westerns on a black-and-white TV in Derby, or from endless miles across desert scrub, or from songs half-heard on radios in roadside diners. The lyric went like this:

When the last Buffalo has gone,
and the medicine man has come undone;
The barnstormer touches down;
the train is westward bound.
Where Geronimo has quit the show,
John Wayne never made the Alamo.
Ghost dancers dance in vain,
and fires go out in summer rain.

Rosalie, oh Rosalie, would you dance with me,
Along the night at the desert's edge,
beneath the Joshua Tree?
Rosalie, my Rosalie, would you sing a song for me,
About the times when freedom called,
and you walked along with me?

The man in black kneels down to pray,
the Bandit Queen has run away.
They're tearing up the old saloon,
a mad dog's barking at the moon.
Don't bleach out the Kodachrome,
where the ghosts of the mustang roam.
Farewell to the last of them,
this is my western requiem.

It was always a strange kind of song, both elegiac and playful. The buffalo and the medicine man: two figures of a vanishing world. The buffalo once thundered across the plains, their near eradication a tragedy and a symbol of how ruthlessly progress was pursued. The medicine man - keeper of stories and rituals - undone by a modern impatience with mystery. Geronimo, who became both rebel and circus act, and John Wayne, Hollywood's monument to certainty: history and myth knotted together until you can't tell which is which.

And Rosalie - ah, Rosalie - she's the one who might still dance with you, who might still sing and keep alive the spark of freedom. The song was about loss, yes, but also persistence. A requiem, but also a love song to a myth that refuses to quite die.

For me, that myth has always come wrapped in music. Not cowboy ballads or hymns alone, but the louder, dirtier, glorious racket of rock 'n' roll. If America was the stage, then rock was the backbeat: a drum kit pounding out defiance, guitars sparking chaos into order and order back into chaos.

It began in the most ordinary of ways. Schoolboy hands on a battered guitar, a harmonium wheezing like an asthmatic bus in the corner of a Derbyshire hall, and the joyous racket of a band who barely knew three chords but believed three was enough. We butchered *Roll Over Beethoven* and thought we sounded like kings. The floor shook not from approval but because the speakers were about to fall over. Still, it mattered.

It mattered because we weren't asking permission. And that was the whole point.

From there it was the Hilton House Hotel gigs: sweaty rooms crammed too full, distortion louder than clarity, the audience stomping so hard the floorboards rattled like snare drums. The smell of spilt beer, the tang of cheap perfume, cigarette smoke curling in the lights - it was intoxicating. We weren't special; we were one of a million bands. But the air was electric. You could take nothing and make it loud enough to shake the world.

Then came the re-education: Dylan's *Blood on the Tracks*, Cohen's *Songs of Love and Hate*, Parsons' *Grievous Angel*. These weren't just records; they were detonations. They stripped me down, chiselling meaning out of noise. Dylan sent me backwards to Guthrie, Guthrie to the Appalachian ballads, Parsons to the Carter Family. Each thread tugged deeper into America's patchwork of voices, teaching me that music was never just melody. It was reportage, prayer, rebellion, seduction - all tangled into a three-minute song.

By then I'd been busking through Europe, learning the hard lessons of indifference and surprise. One night in Sète, on the Mediterranean, Tim and I played for change while the sea crashed against the quay. The songs were ragged, the audience distracted, but for a moment it felt as though the whole coast leaned in to listen. Later, with my own bands, I carried those lessons with me. Not every gig was glorious - most weren't -

but each was real. You learned to hold a room, or a street corner, or nothing at all. You learned that music is a conversation with strangers.

Years later, in Nashville, I stumbled into Layla's and heard the Eskimo Brothers tearing through a set so raw it felt like the floorboards might catch fire. And at the Ryman, Alison Krauss sang so purely that the building itself seemed to bow. These weren't concerts. They were revelations. Proof that music can still tell the truth in a world that drowns in noise.

And somewhere in the mix came The Long Road, my brothers-in-arms, with our 'Heavy Wood' sound. Acoustic instruments played with rock's swagger; folk songs pushed through the grit of an imagined Marshall amp. In our own small way, we carried the old dream forward: take raw ingredients, stir them in a battered pot, and serve something fiery and alive.

But freedom always comes at a price. The same fire that lights up a stage can burn a life to the ground. I saw bands implode on egos and addictions. I saw friends wither from the very chaos that made them brilliant. Sometimes the wreckage seemed baked into the music itself. And maybe that's why America and rock 'n' roll fit so well together: both wired with the same switch that controls the dream and the self-destruct button. Push one and you often push the other.

That paradox - creation and destruction sharing a bed - has been with me every mile of this odyssey. It's in the outlaw towns, the broken dreams, the gamblers and prophets. It's in the whiskey jars of moonshine runners and in the neon signs of Bourbon Street. The American condition, if you like.

And yet - even with all that brokenness - America resists despair. Which brings me to the counterpoint. Because if you want to see despair without meaning, you don't need to cross a desert. You just need to look at the swampy half-light of the internet.

There, young men kill not for belief, not for cause, but for memes. Bullet casings engraved with "if you read this you are gay lmao." Nihilism as stand-up comedy for the terminally online. Not revolution, not rebellion - just brain-wormed absurdity performed for an algorithm.

A survey says more than half of young adults report little or no meaning in their lives. The great enemy is not poverty or oppression, but boredom. Purpose shrinks to a screen; outrage becomes the only currency. It's nihilism with Wi-Fi, and the only thing worse than the emptiness is how *boring* it is.

Contrast that with America - even at its worst. For all its sins, hypocrisies, and violences, the American dream at least *was* a dream. Something to strive toward, to reach for, to argue over. It was big enough to hold contradictions. It had the decency to fail spectacularly rather than not try at all. Better a broken dream than a swamp where memes replace meaning.

One is flawed but noble. The other is just daft and dangerous. If the American dream was sometimes a carnival mirror, the swamp of online nihilism is the mirror smashed altogether - leaving people to slash themselves on the shards while livestreaming it for likes.

Humour, I've decided, is the last weapon against that. My Uncle Bruce was married seventy years, so I asked him the secret. He said: "Lower your expectations, Steve. Lower your expectations." A line worthy of any outlaw ballad or punk chorus. Survival disguised as philosophy. You don't need perfection. You just need persistence. And maybe a tune or two to keep you going.

Which brings me back to the dream itself. At its best, America has always been homemade. Moonshine from a copper still, gumbo stirred in a battered pot, a song picked out on a porch, an invention hammered together in a shed. A patchwork quilt stitched by a thousand hands. Not tidy, not pure, never perfect - but alive.

Perhaps the dream is broken now. Cynicism and anger prevail. But one thing I've learned: opposites strengthen each other. Always. The worst in us can bring out the best. Lawmen become outlaws, outlaws become lawmen. Failure is not the end - it's just the next verse.

That, in the end, is the lesson of the American dream: not perfection, but reinvention. Not the absence of failure, but the stubborn possibility of renewal. Like music. Like stories. Like our own stumbling lives.

So here I am, strumming the final chord. A requiem, yes. But not only for what has been lost. Also for what refuses to die. The dream battered and bowed, mocked by cynics, corrupted by plutocrats, but still flickering in the music, in the movies, in the small rooms where people gather to listen, in the kid who plugs in a guitar in a garage and makes the world rattle.

The buffalo are gone, the saloons are torn down, the ghosts wander restlessly. But somewhere, Rosalie is still singing. Somewhere, Springsteen is still on stage. Cohen still whispers from the speakers. Somewhere, a songwriter scribbles truth on a napkin in a motel room.

Somewhere, the dream breathes on.

This is my Western Requiem.

Acknowledgements

This book has been a long road - in every sense - and I owe more thanks than I can easily express.

To Rob McHale, the fine North Carolina songwriter with whom I've shared songs, stories, and late nights on the porch - your friendship and music have kept my compass true.

To Professor Patrick Allitt, the Cahoon Family Professor of American History at Emory University, and an old school friend, whose conversation and deep knowledge of America's past have often illuminated my understanding of its present.

To Dr Michael J. Apter and Dr Mitzi Desselles, whose friendship and hospitality over the years have been a constant reminder that curiosity and kindness make the best travelling companions.

To Peter Schwartz, an old university friend who somehow combined the best of East and West Coast in one generous character, and who first helped me glimpse the paradoxical beauty - and heartbreak - of the American dream as it unfolds.

To all the wonderful, sometimes weird, often wise people I travelled along this road with; those who shared their stories, their time, a stage, or just a moment of connection. You gave this journey its heart.

To my travelling companions Christopher "The Bishop" Lydon and Kev Moore, for sharing their love of Americana with me and allowing their own adventures to intertwine with mine.

Kev, thank you for the inspiration of your own pilgrimage along the blues highway.

Chris, thank you for being the master craftsman who helped shape this book into something solid and true - a real thing you can hold in your hands.

Thanks to Alan Fernihough for the wonderful cover art that catches the spirit of the road

Thanks to Orla for simply being there, true and encouraging.

And finally, heartfelt thanks to all those who pre-purchased this book, believing in it before it was even finished. Your faith and generosity helped bring *Gone to Look for America* into being - and for that, I am deeply grateful.

To all of you - friends, fellow travellers, and kind strangers - thank you for walking a while with me. This book belongs to you as much as it does to me.

About the author

Steve Bonham

Steve is a singer-songwriter and folk musician with a deep love for Americana and a gift for storytelling. A seasoned performer, he has appeared at clubs and festivals across the UK and the United States for many years. He has released multiple solo albums and is a proud member of the legendary band The Long Road. His music – often rooted in place, memory, and identity – has earned hundreds of thousands of streams. Among his notable works are evocative songs inspired by his off-grid treks through forgotten places, off the tourist trail.

In addition to his musical work, Steve is an accomplished writer for the stage. His musical 'How to Survive and Thrive in an Impossible World – with a piano!' enjoyed a successful three-week run at the Edinburgh Festival Fringe and more appearances around the country, including Brighton Fringe. He often performs alongside his long-time creative partner, pianist, arranger, and producer Christopher 'The Bishop' Lydon.

Steve is also a published author, with several books to his name. These include *How to Survive and Thrive in an Impossible World*, on which the aforementioned show is based, *A Beautiful Broken Dream*, which chronicles his journey through the southern United States, and *Stumbling Over Eden*, detailing an ambitious walk from the peaks of Morocco's High Atlas Mountains to the edge of the Sahara Desert. In 2024, he released his children's book *The Spirit Dog*, accompanied by a tour of schools and libraries across England, supported by Arts Council England.

Outside of the arts, Steve is an award-winning psychologist who has worked across the globe – in Asia, the Middle East, Europe, North America, and South America – focusing on leadership and team performance, conflict resolution, and wellbeing. He is also a sought-after speaker at conferences, festivals, and public events, bringing insight, humour, and humanity to everything he does.

stevebonham.net

Photograph by Colin McMahon

Other books by the author

Available from **artisan-creative.com**

How to Survive and Thrive in an Impossible World

Steve Bonham invites you not just to survive - but to flourish amid uncertainty. Drawing on his life as psychologist, adventurer and vagabond philosopher, this practical guide challenges conventional self-help and calls on you to reclaim your innate resilience, embrace your ever-evolving self, and meet the chaos of today with curiosity, courage and joy. Through vivid storytelling, playful mischief and grounded insight, Bonham shows how thriving in a wild world means loosening the grip on old maps and learning to live on your own brave terms. A bold invitation to rethink what it means to live well now.

> *"Warm, wise and very funny!"*
> - Cilian Fennell, award-winning TV producer and consultant

> *"Engaging, thought provoking and fun."*
> - Laura Burchill The Psychologist'

Stumbling Over Eden

Starting with the simple but quite crazy idea to walk from the top of the Atlas Mountains into the Sahara Desert a distance of 540km, this is a tale of companionship, exploration, self-discovery, and freedom. It is also about the beautiful almost mystical resonance that occurs when you submerge yourself into a landscape. This tale involves the search for a lost tribe of dwarves, discovering the lair of old warlords and an almost mythical Krupp cannon, travelling with a spirit dog, and finding Eden. It is a book for anyone with an adventurous heart.

> *"A boy's own – and girls! – adventure of a trek, from the High Atlas Mountains, across the Anti Atlas, then following the exotic river Draa into the Sahara. You will fall into a world and people as fascinating and friendly as any fairy tale."*
> - Mike McHugo

A Beautiful Broken Dream

A 'trail book' of a journey mostly on foot through the great forests of the southern states of the US and then a trip along music road, from Ashville to Nashville and New Orleans Endeavouring to avoid irritable bears, rattlesnakes, agitated natives, over-exuberant creeks, and a whole variety of other challenges, this is a journey into the heart of Appalachia and the Southern States and the music that flows from it. What emerges is a wry, funny, provocative, and highly personal view of this land and the 'truth' it holds for all of us.

A Little Nostalgia For Freedom

Steve Bonham invites everyone to consider again their own responses to some of life's big challenges: why many of us never quite do what we what we mean to do; why, when so often we are comfortable, do we feel restless; how do we respond to sheer paradox of existence and flourish!

"Perhaps the ultimate question of life is 'when do we fit in, and when do we fall out?'"

In doing this as he takes on us on a journey through the pirate towns of Morocco, the Atlas Mountains, to London, Hong Kong, and the Sahara in search of the source of and the resolution to this, our Little Nostalgia for Freedom.

The Spirit Dog

Written by Steve Bonham.
Illustrated by Tasia Graham.

A heartwarming and true story about a mysterious dog named Black who adopts author Steve Bonham and his friend Moha as they journey through the High Atlas Mountains towards the Sahara Desert. Through the heat, rocky mountains and deep valleys, encountering deserted kasbahs, streams of salt water, remote villages, a young snake, and packs of wild dogs, this is an enchanting and haunting tale of adventure and companionship.

> *"A touching true story about friendship, love and how one dog united a group of travellers on a perilous adventure through the Atlas Mountains. A fantastic read."*
> - Maisie, aged nine

More at **thespiritdog.life**

Artisan Creative
Books | Recordings | Performance

About Artisan Creative

Celebrating the extraordinary stories of ordinary folk.

We believe in the 'artisan values' of craft, inspiration, authenticity, and the love of the raw materials.

Artisan Creative was created to provide a platform for developing distinctive books, recordings, and performances.

> We have performances and workshops available based on various themes and ideas, including *How to Survive and Thrive in an Impossible World – with a piano!*, *Gone to Look For America*, *Stumbling Over Eden* and *The Spirit Dog*.
>
> We've toured performances, workshops and shows across the country, in theatres, festivals, arts centres, community settings, libraries, schools, colleges and rural venues.
>
> Perhaps you have a venue or community setting that we could bring our unique performances to?
>
> Find out more at **artisan-creative.com**

Hear the songs behind the stories

Music runs through this book like a hidden trail. Many of the lyrics you've met along the way began life as songs written and recorded by **Steve Bonham and The Long Road** - the band of friends who have travelled, played, and adventured together for years: Steve Bonham, Kev Moore and Christopher Lydon.

STEVE BONHAM AND
THE LONG ROAD

thelongroadband.net

If you'd like to hear the tracks that are so intrinsically linked to the stories in these pages, you can listen here:

arcr.uk/gtlfamusic

Printed in Dunstable, United Kingdom

72800374R00107